INSTRUMENT OF PEACE

INSTRUMENT OF PEACE
Personal And Spiritual Goal Of The Priest

* *
* *

REV. DOUGLAS J. MORIN

ALBA · HOUSE   NEW · YORK

SOCIETY OF ST. PAUL, 2187 VICTORY BLVD., STATEN ISLAND, NEW YORK 10314

Library of Congress Cataloging-in-Publication Data

Morin, Douglas J.
    Instrument of peace.

        1. Catholic Church — Clergy — Religious life.
2. Priests — Religious life.   I. Title.
        ISBN 0-8189-0551-4
        BX1912.5.M67   1989
        248.8'92   88-34961

Designed, printed and bound in the United States of
America by the Fathers and Brothers of the
Society of St. Paul, 2187 Victory Boulevard,
Staten Island, New York 10314, as part of their
communications apostolate.

Printing Information:

Current Printing - first digit   1   2   3   4   5   6   7   8   9   10   11   12

Year of Current Printing - first year shown
   1989   1990   1991   1992   1993   1994   1995   1996

To Bess

FOREWORD

*
* *

THESE PAGES ARE WRITTEN for my brother priests. They are intended to offer various suggestions and insights that I have myself received in my few short years of priesthood.

I use certain terms with specific, and more contemporary than traditional, understanding. I see meditation as referring both to the period of time spent in silent prayer, and the type of silent prayer which is the mental process of thinking about God or holy things. The words contemplation and contemplative refer to prayer of the heart, not the more traditional understanding, a specific lifestyle of certain religious communities devoted to prayer. Mystical prayer is that uncommon union with God in prayer which is God's action, an illumination or infusion of divine grace.

That some lay people may read this is probable. But I ask that as you read to consider that I write as if in conversation with other priests. I believe the fraternity of priesthood allows me to be rather frank. Overstatement is obviously not intended to scandalize.

Our calling as priests to an active ministry implies an ongoing transformation in holiness. Inactive (or quiet) prayer is one avenue to achieving this. It is God's action, but we must dispose ourselves to it.

Father Doug Morin
Easter, 1988

CONTENTS

INSTRUMENT OF PEACE
Personal And Spiritual Goal Of The Priest

CHAPTER ONE

PRAYER AND SPIRITUAL GROWTH

Peace

Lord, make me an instrument of your peace,
　　Where there is hatred, let me sow love.
　　Where there is injury, pardon.
　　Where there is doubt, faith.
　　Where there is darkness, light.
　　Where there is sadness, joy.

O Divine Master,
Grant that I may not so much seek
　　To be consoled as to console;
　　To be understood, as to understand;
　　To be loved as to love.
For it is in giving that we receive.
　　It is in pardoning that we are pardoned.
　　It is in dying that we are born to eternal life.

THE PEACE PRAYER of St. Francis is an ideal for the spiritual
heart of a priest. It speaks of being an instrument used by
Christ, and of bringing the love, pardon, faith, light and joy

of Christ to those who so desperately need him. It speaks of selflessness and service; of consoling, understanding, loving, giving, pardoning and dying. Lastly, it speaks of eternal life, the ultimate focus of the priesthood.

St. Francis himself was not an ordained priest. But we find in his life and prayer a great example of the spiritual union with God necessary for priestly holiness. His suffering, his zeal, his humility were all expressions of his love for God. So too must the suffering, zeal and humility of every priest be.

The priest is a human being making Christ present to his people through the Church. To be a priest is to be an instrument of Christ for the dispensing of his grace. Christ can overcome any deficiency in human nature. Yet, making Christ present through his priests is not properly done unless the priest himself keeps up vigilant efforts in striving to imitate the one he represents. A priest who does not act with charity, patience, forbearance and depth is not representing Christ as fully as he could be represented. A priest who does not keep his heart set on Greater Things cannot effectively transform the hearts of Christ's flock. We priests have a great responsibility to be ''other Christs'' in thought, word and deed. Without a deeply spiritual interior life, we are almost useless. Without inner union with God, a priest is a mere functionary whose work may be an obstacle to the grace of Christ, rather than an instrument of it.

One of the greatest example from literature of priestly humility and love is found in Victor Hugo's *Les Miserables*. The character of Monseigneur Bienvenu, the Bishop of Digne, is Hugo's fictional concept of perfection in pastoral sanctity and charity. He has opened his door, set his table and made a clean bed for Jean Valjean, a notorious criminal. When the criminal becomes almost frightened with gratitude, the humble priest:

Touched his hand gently and said, ''You didn't have to tell me who you are. This is not my house; it is Christ's. It does not ask any guest his name but whether he has an affliction. You are suffering; you are hungry and thirsty; you are welcome. And don't thank me; don't tell me that I am taking you into my house. This is the home of no man, except the one who needs refuge. I tell you, a traveler, you are more at home here than I; whatever is here is yours. Why would I have to know your name? Besides, before you told me, I knew it.'' The man opened his eyes in surprise. ''Really? You knew my name?'' ''Yes,'' answered the bishop, ''your name is my brother.'' (p. 76)

Hugo attempts to demonstrate how Christ himself would run his home. How different his priestly stewards must seem in comparison. How far we have to go. We who represent Christ can only wince at the vast disparity we must recognize between the way we live our lives and the way Christ himself would live them. It is that gap which we must constantly seek to close. We, as priests of God, must struggle to be more like Christ.

This is our spiritual growth. By closer union with God we conform more and more to his Image, and become more like him. He is no great secret; not has he removed himself far from us. The path to union and likeness is not an easy one, but it is to be our spiritual journey, our pilgrimage. Priests, as leaders of God's people, as representatives of Christ, have the responsibility to be most diligent in seeking him. We must be men of God. If we are not, we have failed in our primary duty. If we are, we must constantly endeavor to make that oneness deeper. Ultimately, as instruments of God's peace, we embody pastoral holiness with such love and humility that one would think our lives were modeled on Christ.

Meditation and Union with Christ

WE PRIESTS NEED a close, intimate relationship with God. We need an intense interior life. If we are to even attempt fulfilling our responsibilities as priests, we must begin with the groundwork: becoming men of God. Even more, if we are to be happy and motivated, it must be due to an authentic connection between ourselves and Christ, whose priesthood we live. As I see it, there are only two ways of this happening: being knocked off our horses like Saul, or coming to know Christ through years of daily, prayerful meditation.

The spiritual life is life, our whole life. As such, everything we are, and do, should be considered a part of our spiritual life. But, like organic life, its growth comes from the frequent nourishment we give our spirits throughout the day. With the body, the better the nourishment, the healthier the body. With the spirit, the better the prayer and meditation, the deeper the spirit. Priests must be especially keen on this. To espouse a life dedicated to God without having the proper spiritual nourishment, would be more foolish than an athlete refusing to eat. Living the life of a man of God must encompass everything necessary for that life.

The frequent nourishment of our spiritual life throughout the day is my concern here. Our spirits are sustained in many ways. Various forms of prayer, administering the sacraments, the many and varied pastoral duties, our reading and devotion, even our recreation, all can be nourishing to our spirits. Some of these ways, however, are more specifically directed toward deepening our union with God. The greatest of these is meditation. (One may be inclined to bristle at that statement thinking that the Eucharist is the greatest source of union with God. In our way of thinking it certainly is. The **Eucharist is the pre-eminent source of grace and union with**

Christ. Grace is God's action in establishing and building a relationship with one of his creatures. Here, however, I am interested in the part *we* have in building our union with God.)

Meditation has been described and defined by many spiritual fathers and mothers. Throughout history and in our own time there have been about as many descriptions as there are people describing. Even realizing that I may just be adding to the confusion of so many varied notions of meditation, I would like to offer my own description of what meditation is: it is spending time alone with God; being quietly unoccupied, with the purpose of closer union with him. It may involve a mental process such as Ignatius Loyola offers. It may involve a method of breathing or posture. Whatever meditation is, it is *at least* the spending of time with God.

Some will tell you that in meditation a conscious or sensible awareness of God is not important. Others will say that unless you are consciously keeping your mind focused on God you are wasting your time. They maintain that it is either thinking, or not thinking. The truth lies between the two. The important factor remains the same: time set aside for God. The *way* one meditates should be as unique as the individual meditating. It is one person alone with God. Whatever frame of mind or method of raising that mind to God one prefers, the result should be the same. *That* one meditates, not *how*, is the key.

So method is secondary in meditation. The many methods can be very helpful, for some people almost necessary. But they are methods which, like educational or clinical methods, are only a service to the primary concern. The primary concern is God. Being in his presence. Taking time for God. Sitting or kneeling before the Blessed Sacrament.

Over the years I have established a pattern of meditation that suits me — you can find your own; for example, each morning sitting before the Blessed Sacrament for thirty minutes to an hour. My meditation has one primary criterion: that I stay there for the intended amount of time. What happens during that time is left up to God. (Often I find myself unconsciously doing something, and may have to add on the time lost. I try to make it thirty minutes of time for God.) This may, at times, involve a great deal of mental distraction in prayer, which is natural enough. But as long as the time is spent with God, not "doing" anything (not reading, praying the rosary, fixing the nearby candle or chair) it can be considered meditation time. I have tried many methods such as breathing and concentration exercises, posture and relaxing methods. The result is that I have continued none of them. After a while — years — it gets considerably easier. I enjoy it.

Quieting the mind and heart, though difficult, is the best way to meditate. God can speak much more easily to a quiet heart. Yet, quiet or not, a persevering heart that offers itself to God every day in prayerful meditation is going to hear him eventually.

There are probably few who would say that meditation is a waste of time. (Although I once heard a man say that meditation that is not mentally productive is a waste of time.) There are many, however, who say they don't have the time to "waste" on meditation. Priestly life is very busy. The demands are great. But, to use an idea of Mother Teresa, with meditation we can do twice as much in less time, because *we* are not doing it. God is.

Time alone with God each day solidifies one's life in God. This is of primary importance for a priest. If there is no time of quiet union with God, we will lack depth and quality in all our other prayers and activities, including Mass. If we prepare the soil of our spirits by daily quiet meditation, then the seeds of contemplation throughout the day — other prayers, pastoral work, teaching and preaching — will find root and bring forth spiritual fruit. If our soil is activity only, activity is all that we will produce. Examples of this go back through the history of the Church to the time of Our Lord himself. Without meditation our priestly life runs the risk of being lifeless or abstract. We cannot be men of God unless we give our spirits time to be with him, to be conformed to him by his hidden grace.

We sit before him, subject to his Spirit, so that he can turn our *knowledge* of him into an *experience* of him. Meditation is not coming to know *about* Christ Jesus, it is coming to *know* him. It is experiencing the presence of the Unknown. It is seeking the One within.

"Be still and know that I am God." (Ps 46:11)

"Joyfully let us drink the sober drunkenness of the Spirit." Monastic Breviary

"The Lord is in his holy temple; let all the earth keep silence before him." (Hab 2:20)

This keeping silent before God, seeking him deep within, is contemplation. It is pushing prayer from our minds down to our hearts. It is not thinking about God so much as loving him, and experiencing his loving presence.

Abandonment To God — Traditional Spirituality

A beginner must think of himself as of one setting out to make a garden in which the Lord is to take His delight, yet in soil most unfruitful and full of weeds. His majesty uproots the weeds and will set good plants in their stead.

Let us suppose that this is already done — that a soul had
resolved to practice prayer and has already begun to do so.
We have now, by God's help, like good gardeners, to make
these plants grow, and to water them carefully, so that they
may not perish, but may produce flowers which shall send
forth great fragrance to give refreshment to the Lord
of ours, so that He may come into the garden to take His
pleasure and have His delight among these virtues.
(*The Way of Perfection*, Teresa of Avila, p. 127)

We realize the need for contemplative union with God. It
is the becoming what we are as priests of Jesus Christ. And we
know that union is experienced through quiet time alone with
God. Can we go a step further, using the guidance of the saints
and other mystics, to attempt an understanding of what we
should be finding in a more profound experience of God's
Spirit? Faith deepens. Virtue increases. Sanctity colors the
simple daily tasks. Most important, God is able to work his
peace through us more effectively. We become instruments of
that peace.

Closing our eyes to this world, we open them on God
within. All are called — especially those whose lives are
dedicated to the service of bringing God's grace to his people
through the sacraments. The call is inward, toward God. It is a
transformation of our human notions of God in an effort to
seek the Truth of who and what God is.

Today the trend in America is a movement toward a more
traditional spirituality. (cf. "Trends in American Spirituality" by Bishop Edward Egan, *Origins*, Oct. 23, 1986.) St.
Teresa of Avila and St. John of the Cross, Spanish mystics of
the Counter Reformation, are prime examples of ones who
practiced this traditional spirituality. In poetic and highly
symbolic language they speak of spiritual heights and experiences which transcend ordinary language. Other examples of

this traditional spirituality can be seen in the Desert Fathers and in *The Cloud of Unknowing*.

To attempt a detailed discussion of mystical spirituality would be nearly impossible here. There is such a wealth of this kind of material and experience in our Catholic Tradition, that only an encyclopedia of spiritual mystics could give a detailed presentation. Yet, allow me to offer a general overview.

Reginald Garrigou-Lagrange, O.P. offers "A brief outline of the main principles of Ascetical and Mystical Theology" in his book, *The Three Ways of the Spiritual Life*. Those three ways are the Purgative Way (ridding ourselves of ourselves before God), the Illuminative Way (when one receives God's light, such as the apostles did at Pentecost) and the Unitive Way (the mystical union of complete Oneness with God).

Most of us earthlings are unable to fly into the heights of God and so we are concerned with the first way, the Purgative Way. It is the conversion to selflessness. It is to become so enwrapt in God that the self is truly revealed. Thomas Merton calls this the "true self." The true self is a frequent theme in his writing.

> The secret of my identity is hidden in the love and mercy
> of God. But whatever is in God is really identical with
> Him, for his infinite simplicity admits no division and no
> distinction. Therefore, I cannot hope to find myself any-
> where except in Him. Ultimately the only way that I can be
> myself is to become identified with Him in whom is hidden
> the reason and fulfillment of my existence. Therefore there
> is only one problem on which all my existence, my peace
> and my happiness depend: to discover myself in discover-
> ing God. If I find Him I will find myself and if I find my true
> self I will find Him.   (*New Seeds of Contemplation*, pp. 33-34)

This is, basically, nothing less than becoming one with God the Father. No simple matter. Therefore, most of us would have plenty to work at in pursuing this first conversion our entire lives. *The Cloud of Unknowing* makes it a little more palatable.

> This is what you are to do: lift your heart up to the Lord, with a gentle stirring of love desiring him for his own sake and not for his gifts. Center all your attention and desire on him and let this be the sole concern of your mind and heart. Do all in your power to forget everything else, keeping your thoughts and desires free from involvement with any of God's creatures or their affairs whether in general or in particular. (p. 48)

> Fix your love on him, forgetting all else. (p. 48)

Since this first conversion is one of purgation, the idea of the Dark Night comes into play. It is the sense of feeling abandoned by God, and the temptation to give up on prayer when it seems useless. St. John of the Cross writes of the Dark Night of the Senses as a great abyss in which we think we are finding nothing, but are in fact enveloped by God. In St. John's *Ascent of Mt. Carmel* he writes about the unlearning, the complete rejection of the self and acceptance of God's purifying love.

> To reach satisfaction in all
> desire its possession in nothing.
> To come to possess all
> desire the possession of nothing.
> To arrive at being all
> desire to be nothing. (Ch. 13, #11)

This gets very obscure. But it seems essential that those who become spiritually mature must embrace this process of unlearning, of denying the self through deep prayer. In denying the self, we affirm the Divine within us, and bring grace, rather than sin, to bear in our work. We learn to depend less on ourselves and more on God. We learn that the spiritual life is more than fulfilling sacred duties and embracing sacred promises. It is a whole life of being one with the God hidden deep within us.

Prayer And The Active Ministry

HANNAH HURNARD WROTE AN ALLEGORY of the spiritual journey entitled *Hind's Feet On High Places* (Fleming H. Revell, Co., Old Tappan, N.J., 1973). It is about Much-Afraid who follows the Shepherd to high places of abandonment to God. After day-by-day acceptance of the many obstacles and trials of her journey, Much-Afraid reaches the high places only to find that those who had journeyed before her were traveling as fast as they could back down the mountain, in the form of a babbling stream. Much-Afraid is puzzled. But she learns that once one has ascended to high places, and has achieved union with God through prayer and abandonment, one can't help rushing back down to help others begin the journey for themselves.

This can be seen an engaging allegory of what the priesthood *should* be. Through years of prayer and abandonment, searching deep for the life of God within, coming by the way of struggle in prayer and battle against selfishness, experiencing God and surrendering to him, one should *then* choose a vocation of service and spiritual leadership. Our problem is we don't do it that way. Instead, often we decide to serve God without ever having a real experience of his love, without ever ascending Mt. Carmel, the Seven Storey Mountain, the High Places. The priesthood can be a life of service to Someone we've never met. Granted, if we were to accept as candidates for the priesthood only men who have had a deeply religious experience, there would be not only fewer vocations, there would perhaps be none. Most never have a direct experience of God. Yet our priesthood is the opportunity to meet God through prayer and sacrifice. For many, it is the opportunity to receive a mystical experience of him.

So the commission, the charge of making our service a response to a real experience of God, is on those who already function in the active ministry. Ministry that comes from love is better than that which comes from fear or sheer teethgritting obligation. We have to work backward, then, in the spiritual life of the priesthood, by confirming our decision to give ourselves in service *after* having made it. But then, we're in no hurry. We have our whole lives to make that decision meaningful. We can gradually seek the understanding and experience of God's love that animates us into service. You can usually tell a holy servant of God by the smile on his face. The presence of that smile is a sure sign that he is doing what he *wants* to. That comes from having been on high places.

The active ministry is demanding. (If you think it isn't, check yourself.) I don't need to describe the ways it is demanding — any priest could tell you. And it is going to get worse. (A cousin of mine recently told me that the parish he lives in, with over 1,500 families and only one priest, may have to consolidate with another parish of 1,200 families, because there are not enough priests to go around.) There should be no question that priestly life is demanding. The issue, then, is what must we do to keep the onslaught from doing us in. The answer is prayer, of course. But not just prayer — contemplative prayer.

Contemplative prayer is an experience of God. With that experience we not only know more of what it is we administer when we are functioning sacramentally, but we also receive the strength to give, and keep on giving, in the ministry. This cannot be stressed enough. If we give time to prayer — meditative, contemplative prayer — that time is not going to cause our ministry to suffer. On the contrary, it is going to be an even more effective ministry.

The priesthood is bringing God to his people, but it is also bringing the people to God. In our meditation we may think of one person who has died, and we commend his life to God; of another person who is lost, asking God to give him the grace of healing. We think, perhaps, of a married couple who are having difficulty, and we ask God to bless them. If we have that kind of contemplative conversation with God, it stirs our hearts to fire for his people. It makes the ministry real and alive. Without such union God is too abstract, the love we share is too heady, too calculated. To be the hands and *heart* of Christ, ministering to a broken world, we must first have a fire of love burning in our own hearts that brings us to such service.

Prayer makes one, at once, above the cares of this world and yet steeped in concern for the issues that face the world. It gives one perspective in hope, believing in God's final triumph, while realizing the great dangers that face the world and our people.

Lacordaire wrote a prayerful reflection on the priesthood and the active ministry:

> To live in the midst of the world without desiring its
>   pleasures.
> To be a member of each family, yet belonging to none.
> To share all suffering.
> To penetrate all secrets.

To heal all wounds.
To go from men to God and offer Him their prayers.
To return from God to men to bring pardon, peace and
    hope.
To have a heart of fire for charity, and a heart of bronze
    for chastity.
To teach and to pardon, to console and to bless always.
My God, what a life!
And it is yours, O Priest of Jesus Christ!

We try to remain above the cares of the world, but not the people who suffer them. The active ministry is to a broken world. Henri Nouwen calls it a dislocated world. Effective ministries have to be deep enough in God so that the world's fragmentation is overcome.

When we look around us we see man paralyzed by dis-
location and fragmentation, caught in the prison of his own
mortality. However, we also see exhilarating experiments
of living by which he tries to free himself of the chains of
his own predicament, transcend his mortal condition,
reach beyond himself, and experience the source of a new
creativity.   (*The Wounded Healer*, p. 15)

It is the work of the priest to call forth from our dis-located, broken people, a creativity in God, in holiness. And unless we have already reached beyond ourselves, tran-scended our mortal world with an experience of God, then we will not have the slightest idea of how to get others to do so. It is more than a logical conclusion, or a theory. Again, it is a living relationship with a merciful, loving God.

There is no dichotomy between the spiritual life of a priest and the active ministry. Though the exercising of the two may occupy different hours in a day, they are essentially one thing: the priest's life. Prayer, however, is primary. First we must climb to the high places of God, so that when we answer the call to service, to be ministers of God's love and his sacraments, we know what we are about and we have the fire of his Spirit to guide and strengthen us.

CHAPTER TWO

DAILY SPIRITUAL EXERCISES

***

Daily Spirituality

THE MISSIONARIES OF CHARITY, founded by Mother Teresa of
Calcutta, take very seriously the call to prayer. Mother Teresa
says that the Missionaries are "active contemplatives," that
they are a contemplative order of sisters who participate in an
active ministry of God's love. Though that may seem like a
meaningless expression — "active contemplative" — by
observing them in action, one begins to understand. True to
their contemplative calling, they are not living in this world.
One gets the definite impression that their hearts are not here
— as though they have a vision that most of us are blind to.
Seeing God in the poorest of the poor is a good example of
that. And they are very active in their love for the poor. The
spirit of Mother Teresa's selflessness seems to be present in
each community of Missionaries, at least those I have
observed.

This ideal of the active contemplative is an ideal for the
priesthood as well. The difference is, *we* have to take it upon
ourselves to become one. It is not built into our daily

framework. It is not even overtly encouraged. Yet it is the groundwork for being true men of God.

There is a daily struggle, a struggle to be at peace. It is common to all of us, and especially if one desires to be an instrument of peace. St. Augustine writes that ''Our hearts are restless until they rest in Thee'' (*Confessions*, ch. 1). In our spiritual lives, our relation to God is the resolution of that struggle. What a great thing, to each day find the peace that comes from God alone — to color our daily outlook with the light of cheerfulness and love, the tones of peace and joy. These gifts are from God, given us in prayer. For our part, we simply must give him that opening, that invitation to visit our hearts, dispelling the darkness and restlessness. With prayer, each day takes on focus and meaning. The meaning is God's love.

Vatican II Priestly Spirituality

IF ONE LOOKS CLOSELY at the priestly spirituality promoted in the documents of the Second Vatican Council, especially *Presbyterorum Ordinis*, encouragement to the contemplative lifestyle — in its traditional sense — is not there. According to the Council, all our efforts to grow in holiness come from our active ministry, part of which is our prayer. The Council states:

> Consecrated by the anointing of the Holy Spirit and sent
> by Christ, priests mortify in themselves the deeds of the
> flesh and devote themselves entirely to the service of
> men. . . . For by their everyday sacred actions
> themselves, as by the entire ministry which they exercise in
> union with the bishop and their fellow priests, they are
> being directed toward perfection of life.   (PO, #12)

Priests will attain sanctity in a manner proper to them if
they exercise their offices sincerely and tirelessly in the
Spirit of Christ.   (PO, #13)

Clearly, the fathers of the Council see the active ministry
to be the source of our holiness of life. And yet, this is not
accomplished apart from sincere efforts to unify the interior
life by silence and contemplation. They go on:

For their part, priests, who are already involved in and distracted by the very numerous duties of their office, cannot
without anxiety seek for a way which will enable them to
unify their interior lives with their program of external
activities. No merely external arrangement of the works
of the ministry, no mere practice of religious exercises can
bring about the unity of life, however much these things
can help foster it. But priests can truly build up this unity
by imitating Christ the Lord in the fulfillment of their
ministry. His food was to do the will of Him who sent Him
to accomplish His works.   (PO, #14)

Jesus often worked tirelessly in his active, public
ministry. He spent long hours healing the sick and expelling
demons (Mk 6:53-56).   Yet he *also* spent long hours in
prayer, often spending the whole night in communion with the
Father (Lk 4:42, 5:16, 6:12, etc.).

Active ministry is essential to the priesthood. Priests are
ordained with a mission to teach, serve and sanctify. Yet this
active ministry cannot be the sole source of spiritual nourishment. It is only one half of the vocation, the "bringing God to
men" half. Each day we must also bring ourselves to God, in
an openness to the movement of the Indwelling to transform
and truly make of us men of God. Our sanctification and

perfection come from both prayer and active ministry. But the
source of grace is God, and to him we must flee each day.

Daily Spiritual Exercises

I RECOMMEND that the *best* part of one's day be devoted to
silent contemplative prayer. (For many that is the earliest
morning hour before any of the duties and distractions of the
day have a chance to make them anxious.) Each day must have
some of this time of pure prayer, heart-to-heart union with
God. A place that is suitable to silent prayer must also be
carefully chosen. (I find that when I move to a new city I have
to try various places before I find one that is both comfortable
and prayerful.) There will be the inevitable distractions. But
some places will have less. So seek a quiet place.

Such prayer will not seem to be effective every day, and
some days will be more distracted than others. But after years
of faithfully sitting before the Blessed Sacrament, opening
one's heart and seeking one's true self, a transformation will
unfold and one will be more and more formed into Christ's
image.

The celebration of Mass and praying the Office are integral parts of one's daily prayer. The time of day one cele-
brates Mass depends on the needs of the place, of course.
Consequently, other prayers must be worked around daily
Mass. That should not be a serious problem. Praying the
Office and other spiritual reading can be done efficaciously in
a variety of ways. I have found that having meditation periods
prior to these more formal types of prayer greatly enhances
my appreciation for them. (Both the Eucharist and the Divine
Office are discussed in more detail in following sections.)

For a day to be truly dedicated to God, one has to have
within that day a time apart with God to put it in perspective.

Our Lord gave us the example of this, praying all night on many occasions. Prayer and union with God allows one to nourish that deep faith. Without prayer, a fulfilling, active ministry will not come about. A priest without prayer is simply destined for destruction. By each day returning to the source of our lives, especially our lives as priests, we re-affirm what we are about. We open ourselves to an experience of God. We become the men of God we are called to be. And we receive the grace and strength for the active ministry. To be effective externally, we must first have an interior prayer life full of depth and meaning.

Prayer is the life-breath of the priest — a man of God. Not only is it required *of* us, it is required *by* us to be truly men of God. Prayer is basic to our vocation and without it we are missing a great responsibility. Each day, prayer is the medium by which we bring God to his people. To say, "My work is my prayer," is incorrect. More correctly, "My prayer is my work." Properly understood, it makes sense to think that prayer is what we get paid for, as it were. There is nothing as meaningless as a priest who does not pray. It would be like a professional attorney who wants nothing to do with law, or a politician who does not bother himself with government. St. Thomas says, "It is the priest who is the proximate source of the spiritual life of the community" (*My Way*, p. 569). This can be effectively carried out only by one who knows the spiritual life and understands union with God. And daily prayer is essential for that charge.

How prayer and meditation fit into the daily schedule is as individual as the prayer itself. Some people pray well in the early morning; others would rather not do anything in the early morning, would rather not see early mornings. Some pray well as the morning wears on; others are too busy at that time. Some pray well in the afternoon, though I think many are too drowsy in the afternoon to pray. Some like the evenings, or late in the day for prayer. Well, the point is clear. Though the time of day will vary from priest to priest, one thing remains constant. It does take time. One cannot expect to fit a day's spiritual exercises into a small fraction of one's day. On a practical level, I believe a priest should be in prayer no less than two hours each day. This includes saying Mass, the Office, and the prayerful preparation and thanksgiving for them (combined total of no less than an hour), meditation and scriptural and spiritual reading (no less than an hour), and other prayers such as the rosary, a spiritual journal, and the stations added onto those.

There will be days on which this will be an impossible ideal. But those should be the exceptional days (such as vacation time, perhaps an exceptionally busy Sunday or an occasional day which slips by in activity). We have to establish general patterns of prayer that will become so much a part of our daily schedule that it would take a really exceptional day to have us neglect our prayers.

Daily Meditation

I HAVE SPOKEN in Chapter One about the need for meditation, and that methods of meditation are secondary to the meditation itself. I would like to go into more detail about the ideal of meditation in daily prayer.

> The Spirit too helps us in our weakness, for we do not know how to pray as we ought; but the Spirit himself makes intercession for us with groanings that cannot be expressed in speech. He who searches hearts knows what the Spirit means, for the Spirit intercedes for the saints as God himself will. (Rm 8:26-27)

In this passage, St. Paul describes the Spirit at work in us in our daily meditation. Mystically, he interprets our desire for union with God, and makes our prayer a prayer of the heart.

George Maloney, S.J., the founder of the John XXIII Institute for Eastern Christian Studies, has written a book, *Prayer of the Heart*, (Ave Maria Press, Notre Dame, 1981). In it he traces the tradition of Eastern Christian mystics and desert spirituality, translating it for those aspiring to be modern contemplatives. He writes:

> The fathers stressed the hesychasm of ascetical practices
> designed to develop *hesychia* or tranquility, both exterior
> and interior. This meant emphasizing flight from the
> society of other men and women, and silence of lips and
> heart by reducing all cares to only the absolute essential
> one, the evangelical occupation of seeking the kingdom
> of God. (p. 31)

Prayer of the heart is the goal of silent meditation, because it is the experience of union with God that transcends the mental or vocal expressions of love for God. It is opening our hearts and inviting or experiencing the Spirit of God. It is a purer form of prayer. As Maloney puts it:

> Pure prayer is spirit-to-spirit communication. It is the
> ability to converse with God in his language of silence,
> to share with him in his Being. (p. 70)

If we are to see value in our Christian calling to prayer — aside from the mere salving of our consciences — then we must learn to withdraw from this world. We must actively pursue the silence and detachment of deep prayer, prayer of the heart. This is breaking away from our self-love in efforts to love God and others more deeply, more fully. We must be transformed in our prayer, and allow the Spirit to do that transforming. If we abide in God, he will abide in us.

> I am the vine, you are the branches. He who abides in me, and I in him, he it is that bears much fruit, for apart from me you can do nothing. (Jn 15:5)

Prayerful union with God is not something only for mystics and martyrs. It is something already within each of us. "In that day you will know that I am in my Father, and you in me, and I in you" (Jn 14:20). The Incarnation of Christ has made us all heirs to the Kingdom. It is in our midst; indeed, it is within us. We have only to ask in faith to be shown the presence of God within us. And we must directly pursue God in silence and detachment. This does not happen overnight. As with any transformation, it takes time and patience.

The Divine Office

THE MOST IMPORTANT PRAYER of the day, outside the Mass, is the Liturgy of the Hours. The greatest advantage of the Hours is its consistency. Day after day one sets aside a certain amount of time to read the breviary. And it takes time. I might even say that the more time one takes in saying the Hours, the more prayerful it is going to be.

There is always the question of attentiveness when considering how to pray the breviary. A priest once told me that he would often finish his morning or evening prayers and wonder what he had read, wondering if he had been at all attentive during the prayer. Then he would go back and reread it sometimes. (He was encouraged by his spiritual director not to do this, because it smacked of incipient scrupulosity.) Most priests would say it usually is not that bad, but that it does require real effort to remain attentive during the breviary. I find this especially true late in the day or when other activities are more present in my mind than the Silence of God. Nothing is more distracting to praying the breviary than thinking about the thing we are planning to do next. When that frame of mind is present — and it often is — much of the value of the prayer is lost. That is the challenge: to combine the prayerful and active ministry.

When praying the Divine Office we should be attentive, as attentive as we can make ourselves. The Divine Office *can* offer us everything else we need (after the Eucharist) for our spiritual lives. That would mean, however, that we would be so attentive during the Office we would enjoy even contemplative union with God through it. The Word of God, the Psalms, the readings, the moments of reflection and silence offer us everything we need for union with God. But it isn't that simple. We can't *make* ourselves *that* prayerful. Such spiritual depth is only a gift from God. But we *can* work at and practice being more involved in what we are doing when praying the Office.

Somewhere between the distraction of wondering whether or not we have even said all the prayers we were supposed to and having the Liturgy of the Hours become a springboard for deep union with God, lies the common level of prayerfulness. Offering our minds and our hearts to prayer, even when that prayer is somewhat functional and not fully conscious, is the purpose of the breviary. And generally we do this. We read the Psalms and prayers, go through the canticles and intercessions, and recite the Our Fathers, all with at least a general awareness that we are doing this in worship of God, and that we are somewhat closer to him for it.

The General Instruction for the Liturgy of the Hours talks about the consecration of the hours of the day (#10). It refers to the sanctification of the priest and his people (#14). These, and giving glory to God, are the very purpose for the Hours. Sometimes this can be very much on our minds when we pray the breviary. But, sadly perhaps, this is probably not usually the case. More commonly we just do as we must, being slowly, gradually transformed by the Word.

One of the most encouraging aspects of the Liturgy of the Hours is that it is a prayer we share. (Once, while praying lauds early one morning, I was struck by the insight that so many were, at that time, doing as I was doing, praying the Psalms for the glory of God. It was a great consolation. I have often thought of this when the Office seemed especially burdensome or useless.) At any given moment, there must be throughout the world — thousands, if not millions, of people praying the breviary. The same Psalms, the same readings from Paul, or John, or Wisdom are being read by so many at the same time.

The Psalms

BECAUSE the Psalms are so much a part of contemplative spirituality, I think a discussion of them alongside a consideration of the Divine Office is in order. I have nothing to say about the Psalms that would pretend to improve upon the writings of St. Augustine and other great minds of our tradition. Nor would I say I have yet a great knowledge or understanding of the Psalms. Yet, the Psalms are the heart and soul of the Divine Office. They are the means of making the hours of the day holy. They are the Word of God on which we priests must be daily nourished.

Thomas Merton wrote about the Psalms in *Bread in the Wilderness* (Liturgical Press, Collegeville, 1953). I recommend that book for a fuller treatment of the beauty and meaning of the Psalms. As a Trappist and contemplative, he was anxious that others realize the depth and breadth of the these great writings. He states:

> For the Psalms to fulfill the function Christian tradition has always demanded of them, which is to dispose the souls of men for union with God, they must not only 'raise the minds and hearts of men to God' but they must inspire us to give ourselves entirely to God. (p. 35)

How they accomplish this, and how we must be open to that movement of inspiration from the Psalms is the theme of his book.

We should seek to pray the Divine Office, specifically the recitation of the Psalms, with true contemplative disposition. As a serious obligation embraced at ordination, praying the Divine Office ''dutifully'' can tend to make us insensitive to the movement of the Spirit within and throughout the words. We may not be paying enough attention to actually be conscious of the literal meaning of a Psalm. How much less, then, do we acquire of its deeper, mystical significance. Merton says:

> Though the literal meaning of the Psalter is sometimes glorious, sometimes bloody, and sometimes simply sensible and prosaic the Psalms have, in fact, always formed contemplatives since the first days of the Church, and they have provided the constant basic spiritual nourishment of Catholic mysticism, along with the rest of Scripture. (p. 20).

The literal meaning of a Psalm may be greatly less significant than the fact that it is the Word of God. As such it is transforming, not simply informing. They can be a daily source of contemplative union with God, of mystical aware-

ness of his holiness and love. They speak not just to the mind,
but to the heart and the soul of one who prays them sincerely.

> Out of the depths I cry to you, O Lord.
> Lord, hear my voice!
> Let your ears be attentive,
> To my voice in supplication. (Ps 130)

The Psalms are poetry because they speak of an experience, they are something more than the mere description or
the words themselves. But they are more than poetry because
they are the poems of God. Inspired by God and written of
God and his people, they transcend any merely human meaning that may be contained in them. The inspired writer was
attempting to express in a poetic way an experience that goes
beyond the human, the earthly, an experience so mystical that
the very words which he then produced are the words of the
Holy Spirit guiding him. Merton says that:

> What is revealed in the Psalter is revealed in the *poetry*
> of the Psalter and is only fully apprehended in a poetic
> experience that is analogous to the experience of the
> inspired writer. (p. 44)

The depth and mystical nature of the Psalter puts us —
when we allow it to — in direct contact with the Word whose
presence was experienced by the inspired writer. This has the
great transforming effect of making us, in a hidden mystical
way, conformed to Christ Jesus. As with the sacraments, the
Word is our spiritual nourishment. The Psalter can even be
considered sacramental, as the making present of God, and
one of the means of dispensing his transforming grace.

When we speak of receiving the transforming grace of
Christ, we naturally see the Eucharist at the center. The

Psalter too can be — should be — experienced in reference to the Eucharist. For whatever particular experience may be the subject of a Psalm, the purpose and response must be centered on Christ.

> We ought to consider the Psalms of the Office as an extension of the Mass, and find in them the movement of the same action which is the Sacrifice of the Mass. (p. 61)

Though the bond between the Psalter and the Eucharist is a mystical one, the link between the Office and the Mass is clear. The General Instruction of the Liturgy of the Hours states that:

> The Liturgy of the Hours extends to the different hours of the day the praise and thanksgiving, the commemoration of the mysteries of salvation, the petitions and the foretaste of heavenly glory, that are present in the Eucharistic mystery, the center and apex of the whole life of the Christian community. (#12)

Mystery abounds when one considers the nature and purpose of the Psalms. Perhaps this is the reason we quickly reduce ourselves to the dutiful nature of recitation of the Psalms in the Office. One day in the courts of Yahweh may be worth a thousand elsewhere, but what is going to convince someone who simply cannot appreciate that? The transformation cannot take place in the heart of someone closed to the contemplative nature of the Psalter. If they are mere words to be hurried through, the Psalms may effect little change in an individual even after thirty, forty, sixty years of diligent, dutiful rattling them off.

The Psalm must be made — in the mind and heart of the man of God — a source of spiritual nourishment.

> Only in God is my soul at rest,
>> from him comes my salvation.
> He only is my rock and my salvation,
>> my stronghold, I shall not be disturbed. (Ps 62)

The mystical poetry of John of the Cross, as awe-inspiring as it is, pales next to the power and simplicity of the words of the Psalter. There is beauty in these lines:

> O Lord, my heart is not proud,
>> nor are my eyes haughty.
> I busy not myself with great things
>> nor with things too sublime for me.
> Nay, rather, I have stilled and quieted
>> my soul like a weaned child.
> Like a weaned child on its mother's lap
>> so my soul is within me.
> O Israel, hope in the Lord,
>> both now and forever. (Ps 131)

How much greater is one good reading of a short Psalm, or even one verse of a Psalm, than hours, even years, of distracted recitation? For the Word to take root and produce grain, it must fall on fertile soil, not be carried away by distraction or choked by the cares of the world. It may seem arduous to plod through the Psalms in the Divine Office, especially when other matters press for our time. But if we truly seek contemplation and union with the hidden God, hidden within the Words he has given us, we must be patient. Patiently we wait for him to unfold for us the mystical, transforming experience of his own poetry.

The Psalms are the songs of this City of God. They are therefore the voice of the Mystical Body of Christ. They are the songs of Christ. They are the songs of God in this world. (Merton, p. 35)

Reading Scripture

THE WORD OF GOD as it is revealed to us in Scripture has a special place in our spiritual nourishment. In the Gospels we come to know Christ Jesus. In the letters and other New Testament books we are given the Truth. In the Old Testament we possess a literature of love, righteousness and God's covenant.

St. Ignatius of Loyola is said to have a simple formula for growing in holiness: read the Gospels. Read them every day. When you finish them, begin them again, and continue to read them. If one would have an understanding of Christ Jesus, one need only read, with an open mind and heart, of his words and deeds as recorded in the Gospels. The Real Presence is just as real in the Gospels when properly embraced — though not physically present — as in the Eucharist, and the effect can be just as transforming.

The Gospels are so important to our spiritual lives. If you have ever asked yourself, ''What would our Lord do in this situation if he were still here on earth and had to face it?'', then you can appreciate the value of the Gospels. I think we often ask ourselves such things, in the sincere desire to imitate Christ. Yet, we must first ask ourself, ''How am I ever going to know how our Lord would act in this situation — which *he* is not facing, I am — if I have not been sufficiently exposed to how he acted in situations he did face?'' The way to come to such an understanding is to be very familiar with the Gospels.

> It is common knowledge that among all the Scriptures, even those of the New Testament, the Gospels have a special pre-eminence, and rightly so, for they are the principal witness of the life and teaching of the incarnate Word, our Savior. (*Dei Verbum*, #17)

All the Scriptures are of inestimable worth, un-
doubtedly, as the inspired Revelation of the Unseen God. All
Sacred Scripture reveals God himself, especially the
Prophets, but among the whole canon of Scripture, only the
Gospels clearly expose the actual thought, word and deed of
the Almighty God become man.

That God himself has taken on human form really is
beyond comprehension. ''He is the image of the unseen God''
(Col 1:15). ''He is the radiant light of God's glory and the
perfect copy of his nature'' (Heb 1:3). ''To have seen me is
to have seen the Father'' (Jn 14:9). Ineffable mystery
awaits us, if we would simply put this book down and pick up
the nearest Bible, opening to the Gospels. You might read:

> You are from below;
> I am from above.
> You are of this world;
> I am not of this world.
> I have told you already: you will die in your sins.
> Yes, if you do not believe that I am he,
> you will die in your sins. (Jn 8:23-24)

Or:

> They came to a small estate called Gethsemane, and Jesus
> said to his disciples, ''Stay here while I pray.'' Then he
> took Peter and James and John with him. And a sudden fear
> come over him, and great distress. And he said to them,
> ''My soul is sorrowful to the point of death. Wait here, and
> keep awake.'' And going on a little further he threw him-
> self on the ground and prayed that, if it were possible, this
> hour might pass him by. ''Abba (Father)!'' he said.
> ''Everything is possible for you. Take this cup away from
> me. But let it be as you, not I, would have it.''
> (Mk 14:32-36)

Our daily schedule should always include the reading of the Gospels. Reading them puts us in direct contact with the Divine Word. They are more than mere words; reading them is more than mere information. The words of the Gospel are Divine Words, and the experience of learning what the incarnate Word actually said and did has infinite implications.

Reading the Gospels over and over will never actually be repetition. Through the lines of the Gospel we come in contact with Christ Jesus. It is the experience of God which makes the undertaking so valuable. It is a personal experience. And that can never be repetition, any more than we would consider receiving the Eucharist each day repetitious. The experience is constantly fed by an ongoing study of the Gospels; to ponder their meaning the way we might ponder the aphorisms of Confucius or the poetry of Shakespeare, yet with the immeasurable difference that these words are Truth.

Christ Jesus is found in the Gospels, not only historically but truly present. Therefore, the Gospels are both informing and transforming for the one exploring and studying them. To be nourished by these words is to be nourished with Christ himself.

> I am the Way, the Truth, and the Life.
> No one can come to the Father except through me.
> If you know me, you know my Father too.
> From this moment you know him and have seen him.
> (Jn 14:6-7)

Continual reading of the Gospels is important for our work of preaching the Gospel of Christ Jesus. Striving to be men of God — to imitate Christ, thinking and living as he did — is made accessible to all in these words of Jesus. Because, like our need for persevering communion with him in the sacraments, and daily union with him in spirit-to-spirit contemplative union, we grow in likeness to him by being in his presence, which is accomplished in opening the Gospels and putting ourselves into them, heart and soul.

I recommend to any who do not already read the Gospels with regularity, to begin today. Read for a set amount of time, or perhaps one chapter a day. Do it for the rest of your life. Start anywhere; go at any pace; jump around if you like. Break open for yourself this great avenue of grace, God's life coming to you through his Gospels.

Daily Spiritual Reading

AS WE HAVE SEEN, prayer and spiritual growth take time. Not only does this refer to the years and decades that pass as one pursues God and is transformed by him, but also the amount of time each day that must naturally go into a serious spiritual life and serious spiritual exercises.

Among the time-consuming aspects of the daily spiritual exercises is spiritual reading. One simply must spend time reading spiritual books. And this time must be set aside each day for that purpose. If we decided to do spiritual reading when we have a little extra time it will never get done. Even the annual retreat is only occasionally a good opportunity for some serious spiritual reading.

Each day there should be, ideally, at least fifteen minutes devoted specifically to spiritual reading. One could easily read and digest about five pages of a good spiritual book in fifteen minutes. Just as with reading Sacred Scripture, spiritual reading reminds, encourages, instructs and edifies. There can be great nourishment to our minds and hearts in spiritual reading. And the more spiritual reading we can afford, the greater will be the benefits we gain from it.

Types Of Spiritual Reading

IT IS VERY IMPORTANT, however, to choose good spiritual reading. (This may be even more important than the issue of time, as hours spent reading a useless "spiritual" book are worse than no time at all.) And we can be sure there is plenty of good spiritual reading, of fantastic variety of style and content. Good spiritual reading can offer us, in the deepest depression or frustration, just the right insight into hope or God's mercy to completely transform our day. It can give us great courage in the face of a difficult task. It can give us the Truth which, somehow, we have been missing all these years about this or that mystery. Spiritual reading is the source of many homiletic ideas and tools for teaching.

Among the many variations of spiritual reading, I would like to discuss five main types: books on prayer, psychology of the spiritual life, lives of the saints, theology, and what I will call "primary sources." These categories overlap a great deal. Many books could be put into more than one category, and some books could probably be put into all five. Nevertheless, these five types seem to exist. Since this subsection of this chapter is devoted to describing spiritual reading, and is a rather practical section in an "impractical" work, I will discuss these types of reading only briefly, by way of introducing them.

Susan Muto is an expert on this topic of spiritual reading. I am not. So I suggest for those who perceive a special need for guidance in this area to obtain her book, *A Practical Guide to Spiritual Reading* (Dimension Books, Denville, NJ, 1976). In it she offers an incredibly broad view of what spiritual reading is available to the spiritual reader, and practical ways to read it. (In her book she does not make the same categories of types of spiritual reading as mine. She groups them as:

Holy Scripture, Essential Reading, Secondary Reading,
Edifying, and Recreative).

Books on prayer are not the most important kind of
spiritual reading. I have put them first in my list of categories
because they are pertinent to my purpose in this book. These
are books written with the purpose of teaching one how to
pray. They are usually short. One of the best, and most
readable, is the classic, *The Way of a Pilgrim* (unknown
author, translated by Helen Bacovcin, Image Books, 1978).
It is a beautiful account of a pilgrim searching for Christ and
''prayer of the heart.'' Other excellent books on prayer are
Prayer of the Heart, by George Maloney (mentioned and
quoted above), *Progress Through Mental Prayer*, by Edward
Leen, C.S.Sp. (c. 1935, reprinted by Arena Letters, 1978),
and *Sadhana, A Way To God*, by Anthony de Mello, S.J.
(Institute of Jesuit Sources, St. Louis, 1978).

Books on the psychology of the spiritual life would include a wide variety of mystical writers: saints such as Teresa
of Avila (*Interior Castle, The Way of Perfection,* and *Autobiography*), and John of the Cross (*The Ascent of Mt. Carmel,
The Dark Night,* and *The Spiritual Canticle*); Fathers of the
Church such as St. Augustine (*Confessions*, etc.); more recent spiritual writers such as Jean-Pierre de Caussade
(*Abandonment to Divine Providence*), and Thomas Merton
(many good books, e.g., *Seeds of Contemplation*). These are
the writers of the psychology of the spiritual life. And there
are many, many more.

A very important genre for one wishing to nourish his
love for God is lives of the saints. Highly recommended for
the parish priest is *The Cure d'Ars*, by Abbe François Trochu.
I think the heroic zeal and sanctity of St. John Vianney is
greatly edifying, as many frequent reference to his life in this
book will attest. *The Autobiography of St. Therese of Lisieux*
is another example.

What I call basic theology — books that speak directly of the Father, Christ, or the Holy Spirit — are needed for the nourishment of the mind and soul. A book on the life of Christ or meditations on the passion can have a great transforming effect. These books are not always purely academic or dry.

Then there are the primary sources of liturgy, ecclesial documents and the Fathers. There is no meditation on a sacrament quite equal to reading the actual Rite — e.g., Ordination. The documents of Vatican II are a good source of spiritual reading and give a beautiful portrait of the Church. The talks given by the Holy Father while in the United States in 1987 are very useful and edifying. And the ecclesial documents which date back to the Fathers of the Church often give a sense of being in the presence of the Truth.

There are both good and bad examples of spiritual reading, so one should choose wisely. There is enough reading material available that one could read continuously, choosing only very good material, and yet never run out. The nourishment of the spiritual life by reading takes place primarily by the Word of God. To fill out one's knowledge of the spiritual life and the Church, however, other reading material should be a part of one's daily spiritual exercise.

CHAPTER THREE

THE SACRAMENTS IN THE SPIRITUAL LIFE OF THE PRIEST

**
*

Sacraments — Encounter With Christ

CHRIST IS THE CENTER OF OUR LIVES. Sacraments are the nourishing of the spirit with His grace. As priests we are both ministers of the sacraments and recipients of them. This is a great privilege. Yet the great privilege may be accompanied by comparable burden and sacrifice. Nonetheless, as we advance in the spiritual life we realize the great value of the salvation that Christ bestows on us through his sacraments.

Baptism And Confirmation

BY THE LATEST STATISTICS (1988 Catholic Almanac), there are presently about 851,953,000 baptized Catholics in the world today. All share to some degree the same conformity to Christ because of their baptism. All are one family in God. All help make up the Mystical Body of Christ.

The sacraments of Baptism and Confirmation play such an important role in the life of the Spirit. They are our initiation into the spiritual realm. No one, ourselves included, can receive the grace of Christ — saving and illuminating — without receiving first his initiation into the sacramental life through baptism. Though our daily spiritual exercises may not commonly harken back to our day of baptism or confirmation consciously, every breath we take in the Spirit does.

The Council Fathers at Vatican II give many beautiful descriptions of the life of grace coming first through baptism.

> His purpose was that they might exercise the work
> of salvation which they were proclaiming, by means of
> sacrifice and sacraments, around which the entire liturgi-
> cal life revolves. Thus, by baptism, men are plunged
> into the paschal mystery of Christ: they die with Him, are
> buried with Him, and rise with Him (cf. Rm 6:4; Ep 2:6;
> Col 3:1; Tm 2:11); they receive the spirit of adoption as
> sons 'by virtue of which we cry: Abba, Father' (Rm 8:15),
> and thus become those true adorers whom the Father seeks
> (cf. Jn 4:23). (*Sacrosanctum Concilium*, #6)

All our spiritual life is founded on our baptism. We are adopted sons and daughters of God because our baptism has made us mystically one with Christ.

And then, as mature Christians, honestly seeking obedience to the Father's will and the building up of his Kingdom, we are confirmed in our love and commitment through a special sacrament.

> The sacrament of confirmation confers a character. By
> it the baptized continue their path of Christian initiation.
> They are enriched with the gift of the Holy Spirit, and are
> more closely linked to the Church. They are made strong
> and more firmly obliged by word and deed to witness
> to Christ and to spread and defend the faith. (Canon 879)

None of this would be brought to bear in our lives without serious spiritual growth. Through prayer we come in contact with Christ, in whom we were incorporated at baptism. And we come in contact with the Holy Spirit who was given to us to strengthen us and guide us. Without prayer these ineffable gifts would be choked-off and die. With prayer they bud and bring forth the beauty of one adopted by God.

As priests we have a special concern to make good the grace we have received. We have chosen to offer ourselves totally to Christ, asking him to make us ever more conformed to his holiness. We have chosen to serve him in his people, to become the ministers of his sacraments. To do this well requires a union with Christ that is not only sacramental, but experienced through prayer. As ministers of God's grace, we must become men of God.

It is a common belief that a parish will be one level lower than the priest who serves it. If the spiritual life of the priest is mediocre, the spiritual life of the people will be poor; if the priest is good, the people mediocre; the priest holy, the people good; the priest saintly, the people holy. Vocations of priesthood and marriage are equally paralleled. The plan of God is fulfilled by each taking his part seriously. The lay people look to us. They need that lesson in living a vocation. We, for our part, cannot give what we do not have. If our union with Christ is suffering, how can we give to our people a sense of fulfilling a vocation before God?

Eucharist

THE PRIEST FINDS the meaning of his life, his vocation, in the Eucharist. It is that simple. Thus the Eucharist must have a great impact on the life of the priest. Certainly it is the center of the priest's life. It is the purpose and source of the priesthood, and it *is* the priesthood, because the Eucharist and the priesthood are the presence of Christ Jesus in two different but united expressions.

To write a spirituality of the priest and the Eucharist would be like attempting to re-invent the wheel. The priesthood and the Eucharist are so intimately united that nothing could ever have been written about priestly spirituality that did not somehow involve the Eucharist. Nonetheless, allow me to offer a few personal reflections on the Eucharist and priestly spirituality.

My own spiritual journey has been graced by God with a modest number of mystical experiences. I do not mean anything terribly fantastic by "mystical experience," but occasions of being consciously aware, in a very real way, of the presence of God or his Mother. Of these experiences, two have been while holding the Blessed Sacrament during the consecration of Mass. The first was unexpected.

In my first months of the priesthood I had heard other young priests describe their great awe at being able to say Mass and confect the Eucharist. But I had remained rather sceptical at their enthusiasm. I considered the mystery to be so great that an attempt to appreciate it in human — even emotional — terms would be rather fanatical or misguided. But my thoughts on this changed slightly as a priest close to me told me of a special grace he once received. He had been given a mystical appreciation for the tremendous mystery and reality which he held there in his hands. It was hard for him to describe, except to say that at the consecration he was more fully conscious of the Presence of God in the sacramental elements than is natural. It overwhelmed him, and he was unable to continue with the prayers for a little while. (One of those attending Mass actually came up to check on him, thinking he was getting sick or something.) It was not an exceptional miracle; the Eucharist itself is miracle enough.

He said it was not even unusual, really, because it was simply a realization of what was taking place. Yet, he said, perhaps it was one of the greatest gifts he had received from God since his ordination.

The Eucharist, on the altar for the Sacrifice of the Mass or in the tabernacle for adoration, is so mysterious that at any moment a priest can be subject to complete loss of faith. Christ Jesus is so utterly hidden in the Eucharist, that we cannot say we believe without having serious trepidation and fear. This can be a great advantage, however, as God remains so hidden under the appearance of bread and wine that we can continue to hope that our irreverence and unworthiness may be forgivable. What depth of faith is demanded for us to believe what we know is happening! And yet, we *do* believe. As fantastic as it is, we continue to live near the Eucharist and believe that — somehow — it is the Presence of God, Heavenly Food, Christ Jesus himself.

In the spiritual life of the priest, appreciation for the Eucharist and the privilege of saying Mass are greatly dependent on the virtue of humility. (Humility is discussed more fully in Chapter 7 under the heading of Pride.) There is something so outrageously humble about the Eucharist, that without the virtue of humility, the reality of the Eucharist is lost on us. I mention this as a sign of hope, hope that as we progress by the grace of God to accepting even the shadow of humility, we will also be given a partial understanding of the great mystery of the Eucharist. We sense in the lives of such men and women as St. John Vianney and St. Therese of Lisieux a depth of devotion to the Eucharist that inspires us. (''With his eyes steadily fixed on the Host, he prayed and wept'' — Trochu, *The Cure d'Ars*, p. 228). This *must* come from humility. The mysteries of God are revealed, not to the learned and clever, but to those in the spiritual childhood of humility.

Cardinal Montini (later Pope Paul VI) writes in *The Priest* (Helicon, Baltimore, 1965): "The Mass and the Eucharist are the root of apostolic vitality, the *raison d' etre* of the priesthood" (p. 89).   If we make ourselves consciously aware of that, we may be more correct in making decisions that affect our time. Taking the time for proper reverence and devotion is only natural when our lives are understood as getting their meaning from the Eucharist. One might be inclined to cut short the time before the Blessed Sacrament, or hurry through the Mass. But we must realize that there is nothing else in our day of more pressing importance. (This has to be tempered with common sense, naturally, that one would not be unreasonably neglectful of someone in need or of an emergency.)

With pastoral sensitivity, Canon 909 of the Code of Canon Law tells us that "a priest is not to omit dutifully to prepare himself by prayer before the celebration of the Eucharist, nor afterwards to omit to make thanksgiving to God." I find that canon inspiring: that even in Church law we find the call to fervent Eucharistic devotion encouraged. It is not an easy habit to get into. Often we have a meeting, a class, or a meal waiting, and taking the two or three minutes of thanksgiving can seem like a great penance. Nevertheless, if we surround our celebration of the Eucharist with our own efforts of preparation and thanksgiving, we will be both more aware of what we are doing and more affected by it.

Tranformation is clearly the key to our appreciation of the Eucharist. It is by hours of sitting before Christ in the Blessed Sacrament that we allow his grace to penetrate our lives. By frequently considering the great mystery of his Presence in the form of bread and wine we gain a subtle strength of faith and conviction. By appreciating the great privilege of the priesthood — saying Mass — we are shamed into humility and gratitude. The transformation is quiet, hidden, and usually slow. But it is there. It is becoming what we are. It is closeness to God and becoming one with him. Christ the Priest, Christ the Bread. It's all the same. Then the words of the consecration take on an analogous meaning for us. ''This is my body, given for you,'' is not only repeating Christ's words to change the bread and wine into his body and blood. Those words take on a personal meaning in the life of the dedicated priest. ''This is my blood, poured out for you.'' A life of priestly service, in imitating the mysteries it is so close to, becomes so selfless and giving that it is also ''my body, given up for you. My blood, poured out for you.'' Priests can take great consolation in being able to appreciate the value of those words of Christ. This is possible when a priest has, in fact, spent himself for God's people. The sacrifice of the Mass is a sacrifice for *us*, especially if we have also sacrificed, and then, we make it ours by offering ourselves — our sacrifices — in it.

As with any growth in the life of grace, it shows itself in action and in virtue. That must be true of the priestly life even more so. Selflessness, patience and service are not simple things, and are not natural to us. I believe that a priest generally does not even begin to develop these in earnest until after his ordination, when he begins serving God's people. Thank God that is also when we receive the great gift and source of strength of being priests of the Eucharist Lord.

Confession

ANY PRIEST WHO SAYS he loves confessions either possesses such a deeply compassionate heart that he has no regard for himself in administering God's forgiveness, or he is not really listening. Confession can be a painful, irksome sacrament to administer. To sit and listen to the heartbreak, the distress, the brokenness of people's lives can be agonizing. It takes such great patience and strength that I am tempted to evade it whenever possible, except for the consolation it offers. To see people approaching in humility the Fountain of Grace is at once cause for anxiety — the struggle with sin, and great spiritual joy — being the instrument of God's forgiveness and peace. The sacrament of Penance is one of Christ's greatest gift to us. There is no explaining the beauty of Reconciliation, the inestimable gift of God's infinite mercy bestowed in the sacrament of Penance.

> The Father has shown forth his mercy by reconciling the world to himself in Christ, and by making peace for all things on earth and in heaven by the blood of Christ on the Cross. The Son of God made man lived among men in order to free them from the slavery of sin and to call them out of darkness into his wonderful light. (Introduction to the Rite of Penance, #1)

Priests must look at the sacrament of Penance in two ways: as a minister of the sacrament, and as a recipient. The two build on each other, and both are part of a priest's spiritual life. In ministering the sacrament of Penance we see the hurting side of God's people. We begin to understand the great need for the Cross, for the sufferings of Christ.

The seal of confession has successfully maintained the trust of the faithful. (I know of no place where that trust has been lost.) This a great advantage, and invites such unburdening that only one who is truly interested in the salvation of penitent souls could tolerate it. Still, I often wonder if all the understanding that goes on in the confessional encourages the minister to seek the sacrament himself. Perhaps our sins are not so glaring, so obvious (though, maybe they are), but they are no less burdens that could be given to Christ.

There is a practical side of confession which is good. To have a chance to tell one's transgressions, have them heard, and to hear the words of absolution is a great blessing. Yet the sacrament remains a mystery. Viewing only the mechanical, the practical aspect of the sacrament, is only scratching the surface. Healing the emotions through the sacrament is important. But it is the healing that the *spirit* undergoes which makes the sacrament mystical. And this is the healing that we *all* need.

After listening to confessions for years, hearing of adulterous situations, hatred, stealing, being away from Mass for years, or whatever serious sin a penitent may be confessing, a priest may begin to think, "I don't really have any serious sin." But the closer we come to the source of light, the more our imperfections are exposed to view. By devoting ourselves to our prayer and meditation, by entering deeply into union with Christ, we will come to realize our great need for forgiveness. The sins which are overt and easily identified, are easily confessed once one is ready to accept forgiveness. But those insidious sins and failures which hide beneath the observable surface are in need of being forgiven, especially in finding a deeper relationship with Christ.

There is something dangerously sad in ministering the sacrament of Penance. Who would not be saddened in hearing people expose their dark sides week after week? The danger is that we may cease to hear. We may shut it out. Sin is a symptom of suffering: loneliness, hatred, emptiness or a need for God are forms of emotional or spiritual illness. This is true even if the sin itself is the cause of the suffering, the illness. The healing hand of Christ is extended to these people in the sacrament of Penance, and *we* are the ones who extend it. If we are not listening, we have lost. We have failed to be that instrument of peace which Christ's priesthood is meant to be.

[The minister] should fulfill his office of judge wisely
and should acquire the knowledge and prudence necessary
for this task by serious study, guided by the teaching
authority of the Church and especially by fervent prayer to
God. Discernment of spirits is a deep knowledge of God's
action in the hearts of men; it is a gift of the Spirit as well as
a fruit of charity. (Introduction to the Rite of Penance,
#10)

Discernment of spirits in the sacrament of Penance
requires a deep knowledge of God's action in the hearts of
men — a deep knowledge of God. A priest must be willing to
steep himself in prayer and seek the forgiveness available
through confession if he is to be a good confessor. The
mystery of Christ's forgiving love is too mysterious to be
allowed to become mechanical or done solely out of duty. By
receiving the sacrament of Penance frequently, a priest can
truly appreciate the beauty of it.

Another aspect of this topic, though perhaps not directly
one of priestly spirituality, is this: the faithful have stopped
using the sacrament as often as they used to. There is a great
deal of speculation why this trend has come about. There
seem to be no good — or at least proven — remedies for it.
Archbishop Daniel Pilarczyk of Cincinnati recently wrote:

I think that one of the main problems we face with
the sacrament of Reconciliation is that people see it not as a
gift, not as an occasion of joyful reunion, but as a burden.
(*Origins*, Dec. 25, 1986)

Archbishop Pilarczyk may be right in his understanding
of the difficulty. People do see Penance as a burden. But it
does not follow that this perception on the part of the people is

incorrect. Should they not see it as a burden? After all, do we not see it as burden? The sacrament of Reconciliation is only properly understood and appreciated in a living and close relationship with Christ. Holiness is the foundation of both ministering and receiving the sacrament effectively. We see, for example, the life of St. John Vianney, who was known to hear confessions for as much as sixteen hours a day   (Trochu, p. 282). In his biography we read:

> It was the holiness of the Cure d'Ars that imparted to his words their power and efficacy; on the lips of other men they might have seemed commonplace, but with what expression he uttered them! In addition to words, there was about J. Vianney something even more irresistible — namely his tears.
>
> "Why do you weep so much, Father?" the saint was asked by a sinner kneeling by his side.
>
> "Ah! my friend, I weep because you do not weep enough." (Trochu, p. 290)

Matrimony

IT IS SAID ABOUT MARRIAGE AND THE PRIESTHOOD that the very thing we give up for the priesthood consumes the lion's share of our time. The reference is to the numerous ways we must minister to engaged and married couples: marriage preparations, weddings, counseling married couples, natural family planning, encouraging family values, helping those whose marriages have failed, and ultimately finding reasons why a failed marriage should be declared null and void. With the exception of teaching, programs and work having to do with marriage make up the major part of the priest's non-sacramental work. In a busy parish hundreds of couples may be undergoing preparation for the sacrament of matrimony. There is some marriage counseling, and even work with annulment proceedings. All this takes time.

There is great need for a spiritual understanding of the sacrament of Matrimony. In the day-to-day life of couples engaging, marrying and living together, the tendency may be to regard marriage as a social, more than sacramental event. The work and goal of Marriage Encounter is to infuse a spiritual understanding of the sacrament in and for married couples. It has proved itself a worthwhile program in the past few decades. But the primary responsibility to view and teach marriage as a sacrament and a holy bond, is the priest's.

There is something of a battle that must be fought here. Traditional values of marriage and sexuality have been abandoned by our culture, and that affects our people greatly. The number of couples of mixed religion marrying has risen to well over half. Cohabitation as preparation for marriage has become common. Even the question of homosexual marriage is debated among members of the Church. We priests cannot just let it happen. We are called to reinstate a sense of the sacred, at least in the minds of those we marry.

St. Augustine's theology of marriage has not yet been improved. His "three goods of marriage" — permanence, fidelity and procreation — say it all. Yet, these are the very things attacked in today's culture. Permanence is lost in divorce (over 50%). Fidelity is lost with affairs (some say over 90%). The connection between procreation and the conjugal embrace has become a secondary consideration.

Though our culture espouses a very unnatural version of marriage (I have heard it referred to as "consecutive polygamy" and "serial monogamy") we can do much to build up the true value of marriage. It begins, of course, with our own holiness of life. By our example of embracing our own vocations, we encourage married couples to enter into the truer meaning of love in theirs. The priesthood, like marriage, is a sacrificial lifestyle. As such, lay couples can look to our sacrifices made in service to God and his people as a pattern for their lives. This is lost, however, when they see in us selfishness or an unwillingness to serve. Our actions will speak much more loudly than any words, whether for good or bad. For this reason, we must be anxious to make our spiritual life the center of our day, our constant motivation. If our motivation is union with Christ through prayer and holiness, it should reflect in the lives of husbands and wives being motivated by their families and dedicated to selflessness. They must see that their vocations come from God. What a vocation is, and how to live one, is not obvious. It is our job as religious teachers to instruct the faithful toward an understanding of vocation, and show them the meaning of commitment by example.

If we want to have good, healthy, long-lasting marriages, we must demonstrate good, healthy, lasting devotion to God in prayer and virtue. This is our responsibility. As Pope John Paul II said in *Familiaris Consortio*: "Families, become what you are." So he says it to us. If we become what we are — men of God — then we can show our families how to become what they are. This we do through serious, time-consuming, fervent devotion to God in prayer and meditation.

Holy Orders

HOW THE SACRAMENT of Holy Orders is viewed is quintessential to priestly spirituality. There has recently surfaced a noticeable shift in the way some priests understand the priesthood. In an effort to play down the hierarchical model of

Church and the image of the priest as an administer of the
sacraments, many priests have begun to emphasize service,
mission and ministry — seemingly in contrast with the sacraments. Caution is required with such a conceptual shift.
Ministry may be the center of the priestly life, in a way, but it
is not the true center. Christ is — or at least he should be. If a
priest were unable to minister, he would be no less a priest. If,
on the other hand, one were unable to pray, to enter into
communion with Christ and experience him as the center of
their life, that person would be much less a priest. Ministry is
a vital part of the priestly life, but it flows out of the center —
Christ. It is not the center itself. Any priest who sees in his
ordination as primary the assigning of a task is going to find
the priesthood a burden. Serving God's people is only possible when one has sufficiently grounded himself in God first.
Otherwise, the work may become merely human and merits
only personal satisfaction — a tenuous reward. The difference is identity with Christ in prayer.

    Let us take, as a contrast to this ministerial focus, the
understanding of the priesthood of Pope John Paul II in his
''Holy Thursday Letter to Priests, 1987.''

> We know that the priesthood — sacramental and minis-
> terial — is a special sharing in the priesthood of Christ. It
> does not exist without him or apart from him. It neither
> develops nor bears fruit unless it is rooted in him. 'Apart
> from me you can do nothing' (Jn 15:5), Jesus said during
> the Last Supper at the conclusion of the parable about the
> vine and the branches. (#7)

> In our priestly life prayer has a variety of forms and
> meanings: personal, communal, and liturgical (public and
> official). However, at the basis of these many forms of
> prayer there must always be that most profound foundation

which corresponds to our priestly existence in Christ,
insofar as it is a specific realization of Christian existence
itself and even — with a wider radius — of human existence. (#8)

In living the sacrament of Holy Orders each day, one
must rely heavily on prayer. The priesthood is sharing in the
work of Christ which is first and foremost to offer himself to
the Father for the salvation of his people. Even the purpose of
the sacrament — making that sacrifice of Christ present to his
people — is itself a prayer: the celebration of the Eucharist.
This is the center and purpose of our lives. For us to come to a
deeper understanding of the full meaning of the sacrament
unique to ordained priests, we must grow deeper in prayer.

Besides having a primary rank in priestly life, prayer
also must be the ultimate, or final, pursuit of the priest.
Priestly life has its share of heartache and longing. We priests
are often burdened with everyone's difficulties as well as our
own. But the loneliness of the priesthood is meaningless only
if it is regarded in a purely human way. If seen as a share in the
loneliness and sufferings of Christ, as united with the cross,
then it has real meaning. For these reasons we priests need
prayer. We need to realize that our work is not an end in itself,
that it is a direct expression of a love we hold strong in our
hearts.

The very acceptance of a priestly vocation from God is a
sign of a desire to love. A decision to embrace the priesthood
may undergo many stages of maturity and depth, but the
greater the prayer and love, the firmer the commitment.

Busy or at rest, we are priests. Active in the ministry or
infirm, a priest is a priest. That identity is a real conformity to
Christ. To become what we are is our goal in prayer. To
become more and more like Christ, in whom we have been
ordained, is the goal we must pursue.

Anointing

Having made the crossing, they came to land at Genne-
saret and tied up. No sooner had they stepped out of
the boat than people recognized him, and started hurrying
all through the countryside and brought the sick on
stretchers to wherever they heard he was. And wherever
he went, to village, or town, or farm, they laid down
the sick in the open spaces, begging him to let them touch
even the fringe of his cloak. And all those who touched
him were cured. (Mk 6:53-56)

HEALING THE SICK consumed a great deal of Christ's time
during his public ministry. The power that came out of him
cured whoever would touch him.

Healing the sick is still the work of Christ in the lives of
his priests, but it has changed since the time of the infant
Church. We no longer look for the miraculous cure or instant
healing. A miracle would be great, but primarily we offer the
grace of the sacrament of Anointing to bring healing and
strength to those who are suffering. (I have often wondered
whether the relative infrequency of miraculous cures at the
hands of priests is God's decision or our lack of faith.)

To attend the sick and dying with compassion requires
real depth and prayerfulness. There is something about the
suffering of Christ and the experience of suffering in one of
his ministers that allows priests to offer singular consolation
to the sick and dying. When one is close to death, or suffering
greatly, the presence of Christ in the person of the priest and
the ministering of the sacraments is of inestimable comfort.
St. James writes:

If one of you is ill, he should send for the elders of the
church, and they must anoint him with oil in the name of the

Lord and pray over him. The prayer of faith will save the sick man and the Lord will raise him up again; and if he has committed any sins, he will be forgiven. (5:14-16)

It is no wonder sickness, and especially serious or fatal illness, is the time of greatest need. There is no comfort like the comfort of Christ. To be a representative of Christ to the sick and dying is a serious matter. It is not easy. It requires that we know what we are about, and have our hearts firmly fixed on the One we represent. We must meditate on the sufferings Christ endured, and be convinced that he has overcome death. Without this we find ourselves wanting. Prayer alone makes the difference.

CHAPTER FOUR

CELIBACY AND PRAYER

**

Celibacy

CELIBACY IS A GREAT MYSTERY. There are so many angles and facets to celibacy in the priesthood that one could not treat the topic completely as just a chapter in a book. For that reason I would like to begin this section by recommending various approaches to the topic of celibacy, and some further reading. With the understanding that celibacy is not the primary focus of this book, but just one aspect of it, I will described how celibacy might be considered as part of the spiritual life of the priest.

Sexual chastity is certainly part of living the celibate life. It is not the heart of celibacy, however, though it is probably the most identifiable of its expressions. The choice to be celibate involves a commitment to perpetual continence. This could be viewed in two ways: considered in the negative it is the giving up all sexual expression (a celibate priest is not supposed to have sex with people); or, considered in the positive as sexual purity (a celibate has consecrated his virginity to Christ). This is nothing new.

On a different level, celibacy is the choice not to have an intimate, sexual relationship with another person. This idea carries over into the psychological, interpersonal level that is so much a part of human sexuality. Yet, the basic idea is still negative — it speaks of what celibacy is *not*. Discussing celibacy from this perspective involves topics such as loneliness and overcoming our natural drive to unite ourselves with others. Though negative, these are an integral part of celibacy, and the psychological implications are serious. One who is unwilling to admit the loneliness of celibacy is headed for trouble. Or one who denies his human sexuality or his sexual attraction to others will find it blown up in his face someday.

Henri Nouwen says about loneliness:

> The Christian way of life does not take away our loneliness; it protects and cherishes it as a gift. Sometimes it seems as if we do everything possible to avoid the painful confrontation with our basic human loneliness, and allow ourselves to be trapped by false gods promising immediate satisfaction and quick relief. But perhaps the painful awareness of loneliness is an invitation to transcend our limitations and look beyond the boundaries of our existence. (*The Wounded Healer*, p. 86)

Anyone unwilling to admit the impact of loneliness on his life, will live a tragic, empty life, stumbling from person to person trying to avoid loneliness by utter dependency. That ultimately results in estrangement and the very loneliness one seeks to eliminate. (And if it is serious enough, this can become a severely neurotic pattern of behavior.)

To help, we have our faith. Faith does not take away loneliness, it makes sense of it. And celibacy is the full embrace of loneliness natural to our estranged hearts. Nouwen goes on:

We ignore what we already know with a deep-seated, intuitive knowledge — that no love or friendship, no intimate embrace or tender kiss, no community, commune or collective, no man or woman, will ever be able to satisfy our desire to be released from our lonely condition. The truth is so disconcerting and painful that we are more prone to play games with our fantasies than to face the truth of our existence. (p. 86)

Celibacy *should* be the refusal to play such games; an acceptance of the challenge to live fully — completely entering the human condition of loneliness. Again, as Augustine says in his *Confessions*, "Our hearts are restless, O Lord, until they rest in Thee."

This is only the beginning. Deciding to live with the loneliness that is naturally ours as humans does not make the loneliness any less painful. It takes a great deal of insight and careful consideration to understand one's self, one's sexual nature, one's loneliness. The work of Keith Clark, OFM, Cap. has been very popular lately in helping people understand loneliness, celibacy and human sexuality.

In *An Experience of Celibacy*, and *Being Sexual . . . and Celibate*, Clark offers his insights about human sexuality, the need for intimacy, the ways of embracing celibacy without being threatened by it, and how to handle the inevitable loneliness that celibacy effects. He touches on some of the underlying psychological dynamics that surface in different ways. Generally, however, he addresses the experience of human love, sexuality and celibacy as he, and those he works with, have seen it.

Clark correctly says that persons who are honest about their need for intimacy and love will stand a much better chance of embracing appropriate behavior. "Everyone needs intimacy. Everyone craves it" (*Being*, p. 41). It is a process

of self-disclosure that feels good because it alleviates some of
the loneliness. Some intimacy is appropriate, some is not.
And unless the need is acknowledged, one runs the risk of
falling into — rather than choosing — intimacy. When intimacy is fallen into, it is probably not appropriate.

Simply put, we channel our desire for union, we control
our sexual drive. Psychologists call this sublimation, and it is
necessary and healthy in a celibate lifestyle. But if one attempts to ignore the issue altogether — pretend not to need
intimacy or positive avenues of self-disclosure — it will come
back at him with a vengeance. Complete sublimation through
denial is a dangerous way to live. It is like a volcano waiting
to erupt, and many are those who have hurt others, and have
been themselves hurt because they did not properly appreciate
and accept their own human sexuality.

Sexual Celibacy

By FIRST RECOGNIZING OUR NEED for intimacy, and the strong
drive that sexuality is, we can then integrate our whole lives
as celibates. This is the positive side of celibacy. To be free.
This is accepting the challenge of loving in a broader way,
rather than in an exclusive way, and so imitate the great love
of Christ. St. Paul puts it up front:

> I should like you to be free of all worries. The unmarried
> man is busy with the Lord's affairs, concerned with pleas-
> ing the Lord; but the married man is busy with this world's
> demands and is occupied with pleasing his wife. (1 Cor
> 7:32-33)

This is a very practical side of a mystical calling. St. Paul
is talking about the dedication to God and service of the

Kingdom that should be the hallmark of the priesthood. And it makes such perfect sense to anyone who is ready to accept it. This demonstrates the need to have the psycho-sexual issues of celibacy and personal adjustment seriously faced: it sounds so simple, but it is not.

We say that celibacy is a gift. To truly believe this is to understand the many human factors of need for intimacy, and the dynamics of human sexuality, but still to appreciate the mystical calling and beauty of celibacy. The loneliness does not go away, the sexual attraction is not diminished. But the gift of celibacy has freed us from the cares of this world, offering us a lifestyle concerned with pleasing the Lord. This, however, presume a spiritual depth that may be sorely lacking.

In *The Priest*, by Bonaventure Kloppenburg, OFM, a noted theologian of Brazil, interesting studies of why priests live celibate lifestyles are quoted. Kloppenburg writes:

Among the numerous crises through which the Church is passing today, people include a 'crisis of celibacy.' . . . Celibacy is felt to be a sacrifice, a burden the priest must carry, but not as something which is a help even in the exercise of the ministry. (pp. 95-96)

And

The thrust of the law of celibacy is therefore that only they will be ordained priests who have made an authentic, responsible, personal free choice of Christian celibacy. In the law of ecclesiastical celibacy, the Church is, strictly speaking, asking not that priests become celibates but that celibates become priests. (p. 101)

That is aptly put. We understand that celibacy is not just a part of a package deal in getting the sacrament of Orders. It is a unique, dynamic choice that must be made on its own right. But this is largely missed. In a study by the Sacred Congregation for the Doctrine of the Faith which Kloppenburg quotes extensively (pp. 95-100), it becomes clear that celibacy is often not even *considered* by many in their decision to embrace the priesthood. It is often even rejected outright.

Celibacy is not a requirement for ministry. There are many avenues of ministry open to non-celibates, and they are increasing. What celibacy is, however, is an aspect of the essential nature of the priesthood. Many will disagree with me on this point. I realize the discipline of an all-celibate priesthood *could* change. (Eastern Rite Catholic Churches have always had married clergy.) But it is my thinking that if the discipline of the priesthood changes, the priesthood as we know it will change.

Perhaps it goes back to the idea of loneliness: being the ''Reed of God'' (the title of Carol Houselander's book) that must remain hollow to be played by the Divine Breath. Or it may be that the priesthood is intimately tied to celibacy because of the availability such as St. Paul describes to the Corinthians (quoted on p. 62). Perhaps even there is something very mystical, very intangible, that we cannot fathom, but which governed the life of Christ, Mary and Joseph and which consistently keeps the Roman Rite Church from changing its discipline in this issue — with little variation — down through the centuries.

Though the nature of the priesthood, as I have said, does not require celibacy (most recently officially reiterated in Vatican II, PO #16), the 1971 Synod of Bishops defined the position that ''the law of celibacy existing in the Latin Church is to be kept in its entirety'' (#90). In 1967 Pope Paul VI gave the modern official teaching in clear, complete fashion in *On Priestly Celibacy*. He cites the various reasons for celibacy:

as a gift of love for the Kingdom; as imitation of Christ; as more complete service of others; as a sign of the way of the Cross; as an eschatological sign. But he also further points out that ''joyful celibacy requires a corresponding asceticism.''

A Deeper Consideration Of Celibacy

THERE ARE, then, many facets to celibacy. There are the negative ones: loneliness, unfulfilled need for intimacy, the sexual drive, and not fathering a family of one's own. There are the positive ones: imitation of Christ, devotion to the Kingdom, availability, accepting the mystical gift, and celibacy as a sign of the Cross and the Coming Age. All these facets of celibacy are observable, external, signs of the basic, internal reality of celibacy. They are mere expressions of the fundamental issue. They are not the heart of the matter. It goes much deeper.

The underlying psychological basis of celibacy is the great struggle and sacrifice within. That struggle is common to all people, but it is confronted and embraced in a particular way by the serious, devoted celibate. Celibacy invites trouble; it is the admission of our deeper alienation. The struggle with celibacy is a human struggle. We face the threat of self-obligation in any intimacy, any deep relationship. In celibacy the risk is even darker, the sacrifice (ideally) greater. We choose to be consumed in being committed to God. There is no affectionate return to comfort the sacrifice as in mutual human intimacy. So we must go deeper. The celibate cannot truly resolve their sexual discomfort, their sublimation, unless they honestly, in the deepest recesses of their heart, actually choose to be consumed by God. The conflict in trying to live celibacy is nothing less than the clash of the human ego with its desire to love. To love one must

forget one's self. In human love there is a presumed mutual
return. But in celibate love, God's return of spiritual joy will
not fill that void of loneliness.

So we are left with a terrible choice. One, to live a
relatively superficial celibacy that sublimates and self-denies
with eyes constantly fixed on the fear of sin or scandal. Or, to
admit that we have chosen to allow God to consume us. The
fear of the latter goes very deep, I assure you. Nothing in our
human psyche wants self-obliteration. Everything there militates against it. But celibacy embraces it — at least it is the
agreement to do so, whether or not it is an informed or
conscious decision.

The celibate seems to stand on the outside of romantic
life looking in. Thoughts of how comforting and natural an
intimate union with another person would be are understandable. Some degree of sexual sublimation is necessary to the
celibate's psychological make-up. There is the unconscious
(at least) realization that celibacy is chosen and sex is not
allowed.

We do so much to compensate. I have found myself
doing some predictable things to compensate, such as ath-
letics, intellectual or artistic diversions, and writing. It is
common to divert a lot of energy into teaching and other
ministries. A psychologist would have a heyday with some of
the defense mechanisms and sublimation methods we use:
denial, isolation, willfulness, hobbies. (Actually these are
probably as old and predictable as celibacy itself, nothing
new.)

The essence of celibacy is not, however, compensation,
but self-obligation: giving ourselves to God. If we go to bed
thinking that here I am alone again, then we have only the
human side of the situation. Natural enough. But if we admit
to ourselves that we have chosen to become nothing — only to
be in God — then we can begin to see the truer, deeper

meaning. Any person who chooses to commit himself to another is choosing self-denial in some way. This is selfless love. But when the choice is for another human person, one can observe the value of the choice. The reward can actually be seen in the other, the one loved. As long as the choice remains strong, the individual doesn't fight the loss of self, but only tries to make the practical workings of it as smooth as possible.

As a celibate and a teacher I allow myself to become very attached to many of the children I teach. This is a healthy and reasonable form of compensation. Mother Teresa says children are the beauty of God. To hug them and show them unconditional love is part of being their spiritual father. They usually respond to my interest in a very positive way, at least the very young. Yet, the love shown them may be an expression of a basically selfish love. It fulfills a need. They do not always think of me as unusual, just someone who willingly comes into their world to love them. I have them to love, and it is all very natural and good. The spontaneity makes this affection acceptable. I am able to give my love, without their really being affected. I do not *expect* any signs of affection from them, I have little fear of rejection. Just having them to love is a great consolation. Whether they know that or not does not much matter. Still, it is not the self-obliterating kind of love of celibacy, but an acceptable expression of affection. It is not untoward, not *wrong*, really, but perhaps a little self-indulgent as a human sentiment.

With God that doesn't work. He is just too big. I can't look to God and say that *there* is the placement of my love. He is love itself, and has no need of my love. So to think of him as loved by me is like thinking of the sun as brightened by a flashlight pointed upward at midday. Such light is completely obliterated. Such love is completely consumed. A celibate person who truly lives and loves completely celibately is nothing. To such a person God is all. He is consumed, obliterated.

That is the immense struggle of celibacy. That is the overcoming of the deepest drive in our human nature, the nature to survive, to *be* one's self. A celibate only comes face to face with this raw struggle after the many onion-skinned layers of compensation, sublimation and defenses have been penetrated (not, need I say, taken away) and the true self is revealed.

Acceptance

LIVING THE PRIESTHOOD IS AN ART, a unique expression of a personal talent. It is self-expression. Every priest is, in a way, an artist, using his talent to bring beauty and effectiveness out of a relatively unrestricted vocation. Each priest lives the priesthood in his own way. There are certain conventions for this art form, certain roles and functions of the priest. But for every priest, how he handles a given situation, the way he teaches or preaches, how he channels the time and energy celibacy affords, all these require the temperament and attention of an artist. (Some may say that the conventions overshadow the art — that a priest should be free to live his priesthood in whatever way he thinks fits. It seems this approach is too vague, however, to keep an orderly identifiable priesthood intact.)

There is a subtle difficulty here, however. Art is only of value when it has come from the artist's heart, when it is an expression of an intangible experience. The art must be consistent with the artist. If this organic connection is lost, the result is second class art at best.

For the priest this requires that he ''imitate the mysteries he holds,'' to quote the words of the ordination ceremony. We live the priestly life. That requires that we are truly seeking God, not just fulfilling a role in society. If one were to attempt the art of the priesthood without honestly endeavoring to imitate Christ, the result would be stagnant and pathetic. There would be little art involved. It would be something more like marketing than art (the substitute for art in contemporary entertainment). As St. John Neumann would pray, "Lord, nothing will happen today that you and I together cannot handle." Each day calls forth the artist's heart. For the priest to be a true artist, his work must come from a deep conviction that it is important work, that the people he serves are important to him and to God, that giving his best, most artful attempt to every task, will effect real transformation in the people among whom he works.

This implies a certain submission from a servant of God. To be an artist and at the same time purely selfless is demanding. The self-expression must be the selfless expression of doing God's will and not our own. The expression of the priestly art must be both self-expression, but also completely accepting of God's will for us. Acceptance is the key. If we can be ourselves, and able to express ourselves in the priestly art, in any situation, that comes from accepting whatever God wants. It is surrender to his will.

Mother Teresa of Calcutta speaks eloquently of acceptance in a film that was made about her life and work. It is a soliloquy that comes toward the end of the film. She says:

> Jesus said that *I* have chosen you. *I* have called you by your name. You are mine. Every day you have to say yes. Total surrender. To be where he wants you to be. If he puts you in the street, if everything is taken from you and suddenly you find yourself in the street, to accept to be in the street at that moment. Not for you to put yourself in the street, but to accept to be put there. This is quite

different. To accept if God wants you to be in a palace, well
then, to be in the palace. As long as *you* are not choosing to
be in the palace. This is the difference; this is what makes
the difference in total surrender. To accept whatever he
gives and to give whatever it takes with a big smile. This is
the surrender to God. And to accept to be cut to pieces and
yet every piece to belong to him. This is the surrender:
to accept all the people that come, the work that you have to
do. Today maybe you have a good meal, tomorrow you
have nothing. There is no water in the pump; alright, to
accept. And to give whatever it takes: it takes your good
name, it takes your health, it takes . . . Yes . . . That's the
surrender. And that is the . . . You are free then.

The priesthood is a life of acceptance. But it is not a
passive acceptance, not simply giving in to suffering. It is
positive embracing of the blessings and hardships that God
gives us. The life of Mother Teresa is a good example. She is
no passive agent in her religious life. She is a very up-front,
knows-what-she-wants woman. She has accepted with zeal
God's inner call to serve the poor.

It is not a partial acceptance. In the same film that has the
words of Mother Teresa quoted above, one of her sisters gives
a simple but profound compliment: "She has no shadows
about her." What you see is what she is: a servant of God with
no variation, no hidden agenda. How many shadows we all
have! Some of our shadows, some of our hidden faults and
sins are such overwhelming shadows we spend all our time
hiding the shadows and completely losing sight of the art we
are about.

We would be so much more effective if we could truly
accept God's call to service, completely, with abandonment.
Like Mary. But instead we are more like poor King David. He
lost sight of his responsibility only temporarily, taking
Bathsheba and having Uriah killed (2 S 12:1-7, 10-17). Yet,

to this day his sin is relentlessly proclaimed in the Scriptures. It puts such a different tone on the life of David, a tone which is so apparently contrary to his greatness in battle with Goliath.

Acceptance means giving our wills over to God. That is the basis of the art of the priesthood. It is nothing fantastic or impractical. But the difficulty is that it has to be daily, over and over again accepting our priestly duties with cheer, "God loves a cheerful giver" (2 Cor 9:7). The Church describes the lives of saints as doing "ordinary things in extraordinary ways." It is unique to each priest, to every Christian, actually. How to live out a relationship with God. The love for God must be primary, not the vocation. Just as the experience of the artist is so much more than the medium used to express the art. The vocation comes as an acceptance, in love to service.

How each one lives the priesthood will be unique. The diversity makes for richness in the Church. But only when the diversity is a difference of style and not of kind. There is no room for diversity that comes from selfishness or sin. There is no room for shadows. Insofar as we allow shadows to hide a part of us, that far have we obstructed the work of the true Artist whose instrument we are. Insofar as we are unwilling to accept what he calls us to, that far have we distorted the beauty and order of his work in us.

The Challenge Of Love

OCCASIONALLY something breaks through the surface of our priesthood which is tremendously sad. Men called to love feeling loveless and hackneyed. With the priesthood itself being such an enigma, one cannot continuously keep up the appearance that everything is hunky-dory. Days come, sometimes just passing moments, when in a moment of clarity the truth arises to contest us. Maybe we come to the realization that we are stupid men on a stupid pursuit. No one is really listening, no one really cares. We seem to have missed the boat entirely. On the one hand, called to sanctify the world, we have become workers in the mechanism of the Church, nothing more. Our lives do not demonstrate the deep sense of the presence of God through peace and patience of unconditional love. On the other hand, we realize the work we do in the vineyard is not really *that* important. God, in his infinite mercy could turn these stones into bread. Do we actually think that our presence *anywhere* is going to do it *for* him? The priesthood can seem absolutely meaningless. It's our own foolishness, our fault. We have deluded ourselves, and lost the vision.

> I tend to gaze quite closely at the faces of priests I meet
> on the street to see if a lifetime of love has marked
> them noticeably. Real serenity or asceticism I no longer
> expect, and I take for granted the beefy calm that often goes
> with Catholic celibacy, but I am watching for the marks of
> love and often see mere resignation or tenacity. (Edward
> Hoagland, ''The Urge for an End,'' *Harper's*, March
> 1988)

Then we start to doubt. Does God really intend this celibacy? The loneliness? The ''beefy calm''? It's an expensive venture for us — it costs us both our all and each day enduring it. Something is not right, not natural.

After doubt comes resignation. It may not be natural, but I have chosen and agreed to it. It may be nonsensical, but I am not going to become an ex-priest. So we resign ourselves to the duties, to the work. Perhaps we throw ourselves into the work to escape thinking about it. If one keeps busy enough one does not have to concern himself with the unanswerable.

Eventually this settles into an acute duality: you know, neither saint nor sinner — man of God but feet of clay. Or perhaps one isolates himself. A pathetic thing to see is a priest who has unconsciously resolved to love only himself. And it happens, often. We are all tempted to this, and many yield to the temptation. The devil wins, ironically. Men of God wrapping themselves with an elaborate veneer of service and virtue to conceal their primary love: self-love. Their little kingdom makes them a king.

The answer, of course, is love — love of God. Salting the earth with our spiritual fatherhood is what we are about. The flavor of this is love. People must taste it in our actions and words. People must recognize it in our faces. If they do not, we have failed. We have not been up to the challenge of our vocation, and have not become sufficiently the men of God we desire to be. Yet, what a demand! No one has the right to expect that of us! Still, if they do there is something there. They want to see the mark of God on our faces, in our eyes. They want to see the scars from wounds of love. They want to believe that someone understands and cares. We fascinate them, and they look to us. If only we could have that kind of love in our hearts — so much that it actually shows on our faces.

That kind of love is from God. It is a gift. It is costly. It goes unfathomably deeper than our priestly duties. It rises infinitely higher than where our feet of clay can take us. It is God shining through the darkness. It is God, and God is love.

CHAPTER FIVE

PRAYER IN PREACHING AND TEACHING

✻
✻✻

Faith Knows,
Life Teaches, God Transforms

THE FLAME THAT ARISES in the heart of one who allows himself to be set on fire by the Spirit of God is no useless flame. The flame becomes the zeal to proclaim the Kingdom of God's love. It motivates and empowers. One who submits to the healing presence of God in prayer will feel that call to proclaim the love of God with his life.

In Scripture this is seen time and again in the prophets of Israel as well as the apostles and disciples of the early Church. Among the Old Testament prophets, Jeremiah was appointed prophet to the nations, though initially he complained that he was too young. Once the flame of God's love was enkindled in his heart, though, he felt compelled to prophesy. Isaiah had a vision of God and heard God question, "Whom shall I send?" "Send me!" was Isaiah's response (Is 6:8). Jonah decided to run away from Yahweh, but was thoroughly unsuccessful.

All the prophets heard the call of God, and that call pursued them until they accepted it and became the mouthpieces of God.

The mysterious event of Pentecost filled the apostles with a mystical zeal: a mystical power of the Holy Spirit that compelled these previously cautious men to go public. Not only do they go public, but with such fervor that everyone "hears them in his own native language" (Ac 2:6). St. Paul, once having seen his vision of Christ, becomes the preeminent advocate of the Gospel. He and the other apostles are silenced neither by imprisonment, nor by threats, nor even by their own impending execution. St. Stephen, the first martyr, preaches from beneath the shower of stones that brings about his death.

Once one has had a deep experience of God's love, one is compelled to become its advocate. Faith inspires us to work for the conversion of the world. There is a natural progression from an experience of God's love to serving him in proclaiming the Gospel of that love. More than a desire, it is a calling — a calling from God himself.

Paul explains:

> Yet, preaching the gospel is not the subject of a boast; I
> am under compulsion and have no choice. I am ruined if I
> do not preach it! If I do it willingly, I have my recompense;
> if unwillingly, I am nonetheless entrusted with a charge.
> (1 Cor 9:16-17)

Once the experience of God becomes the impetus for preaching the Gospel of Christ, the actual proclamation is as unique as the one called. Ultimately, one's life does the preaching. Not by words alone do we show that we are disciples of Christ and ministers of his Word, but by our whole lives. Be confident. One has no need to fear, for the holiness of life that comes from union with God will guide us. Jesus assures us:

> Do not worry about how to defend yourself or what to say, because when the time comes, the Holy Spirit will teach you what you must say. (Lk 12:11-12)

Conversely, even if our words are eloquent — even mesmerizing — if they do not flow from the Spirit within, they will be empty words. With the Spirit, though, every thought, word and action become a means of proclaiming. The person of faith is the preacher, but the Spirit is the guide. And so there is no need to fear — work, yes, but fear, no.

It is God that transforms those who may hear the words of faith and love. There is no accounting for what may become a moment of grace in the mind and heart of someone listening to us preach or teach. God's ways are not our ways. This becomes so clear as one preaches with a conscious desire to remain open to the movement of the Holy Spirit. The truth of the message becomes second nature when we have submitted our hearts to the Divine Will.

As preachers and teachers we often find that the very homilies or classes we may feel are good or even impressive seem to go relatively unnoticed. While occasionally, when we feel as though the thoughts of a particular moment of preaching fail, someone's heart has been opened by the movement of the Spirit and it becomes a moment of grace for that person. It is God's way of reminding us that the work is ultimately his, that we are the instruments.

Our faith and prayer, then, are the foundation of our right to proclaim the Gospel. They are the groundwork for life in the Spirit. Once these are well-founded, we can be confident that the Spirit will work through our feeble efforts. We can be confident that *if* we are willing to embrace the challenge of the Gospel in our lives, then our lives can become true instruments of God's Word. We become the mouthpiece of God when we have conformed ourselves to his Son. And then, by the grace of those words spoken through us, God leads the hearts of his listeners to faith and the hearts of his faithful to deeper union with him.

Preaching From Real Life

The People of God finds its unity first of all through the Word of the living God, which is quite properly sought from the lips of priests. Since no one can be saved who has not first believed, priests, as co-workers with their bishops, have as their primary duty the proclamation of the Gospel of God to all. In this way they fulfill the Lord's command: Go into the whole world and preach the gospel to every creature. (PO, #4)

FOR THIS WE HAVE EMBRACED the sacrament of Holy Orders; to preach the Gospel of Christ. How real is that Gospel to us? How faithful are we to it? As a primary duty, our preaching assumes a principal role in our lives — our spiritual lives. As such, of the many aspects of preaching in the life of the priest — Scripture interpretation, homily preparation, the ''hermeneutic'' — spiritual growth is the most important. Spiritual growth undercuts all the practical aspects of homiletics, and even compensates for deficiencies in other areas. Preaching is imparting the Gospel of Christ. Therefore, it is closeness to him that makes preaching real and effective.

Everyone who preaches has a style. Some are good styles, and some are bad. Some preachers have the gift of speaking eloquently and with passion; others are lucky to avoid stumbling over their every word. Though it may be the deciding element of great preaching, style is not the key to good preaching. Content is. And the content is Christ Jesus.

Some preachers are great scholars and have vast knowledge of the Scriptures. This is a great gift and a treasure. Being able to break open the Word of God with confidence and understanding cannot but impress and edify a congregation. Still, broad knowledge of the written word does not replace the need for depth of faith and holiness of life.

Great oratorical skills can truly entertain and exhort an audience. And it would be a great advantage if every priest were gifted in this. But not all priests are gifted speakers. And even if they were, it would be worthless if sanctity were replaced by pride in their hearts.

If a preacher has something worth saying, his congregation will be very patient with the way he says it. If the efforts to express spiritual notions are muddled or poorly expressed, but the sense of deep union with God is present, the preaching will have its effect. On the other hand, if a preacher cannot speak about Christ from personal experience — because his prayerful relation with him is vague or shallow — yet is able to speak with great flair, he will only impress some of the people for a while, and no one for long. If a preacher is a deeply spiritual person, he will always have something to say. One is effective in preaching if he is interested in having his listeners also become deeply spiritual. There is a growth involved here, a development, that should continue throughout the priesthood. The practical elements of style in preaching become second nature, it appears, after years of weekly and daily homilies. But the mystical element of Christ in a message of faith is always new. That mystical component,

that Presence, must always demand of the one preaching great
devotion to prayer and sacrifice.

There is need for caution here, however. Though deep
faith will shine through even poor preaching and sad
circumstances, anyone whose spiritual union with Christ is
close will always be anxious to be effective in making Christ
known. Such a one will be constantly seeking to better his
preaching ability, his preparation, his knowledge of the
Scriptures. Holiness will not allow one to cultivate bad
preaching habits. On the contrary, it will fill one with zeal for
more and more effective ways of converting hearts and giving
real spiritual nourishment.

The Cure of Ars, St. John Vianney, is the perfect example of compensating for a lack of natural gifts by supernatural
ones. (No wonder he is the patron of parish priests.) It is
commonly known that he was no genius. He had difficulties
with his studies, a real lack of common sense, and almost no
social sensibilities. And yet, by his deep faith and conscious
union with Christ, he overcame his shortcomings. When he
would preach on the love of God, entire congregations would
be moved to tears. Trochu, his biographer, gives us an example of his great zeal:

> Returning once more to the sacristy, he began to write,
> in a standing position, as became one who was preparing
> to do battle for the truth of which he wished to be
> the champion. His pen ran rapidly over the paper, so that at
> times he covered as many as ten large sheets with his fine,
> sloping handwriting. Occasionally he worked for seven
> hours on end and far into the night. (Trochu, p. 131)

The great advantage of spiritual growth for preaching is
even more than the closeness to Christ, the content. Holiness
is never static, it never ceases to flourish, mature, unfold.

The challenge of the Gospel is always new; there is always something new to keep one from becoming complacent. With growing sanctity there is no fear of repetition, no lack of new ideas, no rut to find oneself in. A want of ideas is a symptom of spiritual standstill, whereas when Christ is alive in the heart of the preacher, the Scriptures and the needs of the flock present more ideas than there are homilies to give. (This is not to say that the development of ideas comes any easier.)

The Gospel speaks to the mind and the heart of one steeped in God's love. Just as the Eucharist is the nourishment of the soul through the body, preaching the Gospel is the nourishment of the soul through the mind. We read in the *General Instruction of the Roman Missal*:

> In the readings, explained by the homily, God is speak-
> ing to his people, opening up to them the mystery of
> redemption and salvation, and nourishing their spirit;
> Christ is present to the faithful through his own word. (#33)

Sources Of Material For Preaching

IF ONE WANTS a *practical* guide to the priesthood, or as the case may be, preaching, I am not the person to consult. My experience is very limited, and certainly not largely practical. My purpose here, instead, is to demonstrate the practical dependence preaching has on prayer. (If you are interested in *A Practical Guide to Preaching*, that book is by George R. Fitzgerald, CSP, Paulist Press, New York, 1980. Quite practical; quite good. Another even more recent title, also by a Paulist, is likewise excellent: *Wake Up and Preach!* by James F. Finley, CSP, Alba House, New York, 1986.)

The primary source of material for preaching is the Holy Spirit. Christ is the primary topic of preaching. The primary reason for preaching is to impart better understanding of how God touches the human condition. The Holy Spirit, Christ and an understanding of the human condition are available to anyone. But only through prayer.

Prayer is the starting point and the very heart of preaching. It is the starting point. Perhaps one should begin homily preparation with a prayer of, "Come, Holy Spirit, give me the words you would have me say," or to say just before a homily, "Come, Lord Jesus, and make me an instrument to teach these people of yours." Hours of sincere prayer and meditation over a homily cannot but make the message more clearly that of Christ.

But even more than the immediate calling on God at the time of preaching or preparation, we need to interpret with a prayerful heart the Scriptures, the needs of the people, the signs of the times, the events of the day.

Reading is essential. You cannot give what you don't have. If one's mind is not nourished with new spiritual insights and deeper understanding, there will be little to work with in making a homily interesting. Since I have already gone into the value of scriptural and spiritual reading in Chapter Two, I will not belabor the point.

I was once told to prepare homilies with "the Bible in one hand, and the newspaper in the other." The point may be well taken. It was a stressing of the need to be informed about the issues of the day and the things that affect the lives of the people who will listen to you. Still, this must be tempered, it seems, with an appreciation for the fact that we are not of this world. We don't *have* to know every little thing that is going on in the world. We *do* have to know what is what in the spiritual life. A careful balance is the best formula. But if I were to fault, I think I would rather fault in the favor of the spiritual life over current events.

Still, we do not preach in a vacuum. We are social critics as well as spiritual leaders. It is our duty to interpret for the people we serve the issues of the day, the trends in culture and society, the evils and blessings which are encountered daily. Spiritual depth will constantly call us to interpret the day-to-day events of life in the context of Christ's love. We can utilize all aspects of human knowledge and experience to help our people. ''I have made myself all things to all men in order to save at least some of them'' (1 Cor 9:23).

Our own experience is a key source of material for preaching the Gospel. Its value, however, must be properly appreciated. For only a life that is truly Christ-like can be freely cited as a source of Gospel values. A useful source of material for preaching the Gospel is our life, insofar as it is consistent with the Gospel. Like all God's people, we struggle to live the Gospel. We can draw from that struggle in our preaching. The difference is, however, that the struggle is perhaps more scrutinized in us. All Christians have the responsibility to face daily the Gospel challenge, to interpret the world in light of the Gospel message every day, and to see to it we are honestly trying to put that Gospel message into real life practice. If we are not facing the Gospel challenge, if we are not trying to actually live the Gospel, our preaching will be hypocritical and ultimately meaningless. But, with the grace of God, and in growth in the spiritual life, we can gradually draw close to the One we proclaim.

As Educators

AS WITH PREACHING, teaching is greatly dependent on knowledge and understanding of the Faith. Only the fool would try to teach without himself first having a broad and working knowledge of his subject. Presuming such knowledge, then, we must ask what, more than a knowledge of the Faith, makes one a teacher of the Faith? The Vatican Council Fathers write:

> As educators in the Faith, priests must see to it, either by themselves or through others, that the faithful are led individually in the Holy Spirit to a development of their own vocation as required by the Gospel, to a sincere and active charity, and to that freedom with which Christ has made us free. Ceremonies however beautiful, or associations however flourishing, will be of little value if they are not directed toward educating men in the attainment of Christian maturity. (PO, #6)

Educating people toward Christian maturity is so much more than merely imparting knowledge. *That* we are educators in the Faith is clear. *How* we fulfill that role is not.

Though teaching is a primary duty in the life of a priest, to see it also as a source of spiritual growth — for those being taught, as well as the one teaching — is essential. In close relation to Christ, one finds joy and consolation in speaking and teaching about him. And the message is received (or rejected) with vastly more significance than mere human knowledge is.

To consider a spirituality of teaching one must account for the nature of religious education. It must be Christ-centered. Pope John Paul II wrote in *Catechesi Tradendi*:

> Christocentricity in catechesis also means the intention to transmit not one's own teaching or that of some other master, but the teaching of Jesus Christ, the Truth of all that He is. We must therefore say that in catechesis it is

> Christ, the Incarnate Word and Son of God, who is taught
> — everything else is taught with reference to Him — and
> it is Christ alone who teaches — anyone else teaches to the
> extent that he is Christ's spokesman, enabling Christ to
> teach with his lips. (para. 6)

Though sometimes appearing very common, teaching takes on a mystical nature when one truly becomes the instrument of Christ. Pope John Paul II — who is believed by some of his closest aides to be a man of mystical prayer — demonstrates this in his life. When one is not promoting himself but Christ in his teaching, one is freed from responsibility for the acceptance or rejection of the message on the part of those who are taught. When the Holy Father travels to proclaim the Gospel to various countries, he speaks to all who will listen. He has the responsibility to teach; others have the choice to listen or not. When Pope John Paul II arrived in the United States on September 10, 1987, he said:

> I come to proclaim the Gospel of Jesus Christ to all who
> freely choose to listen to me; to tell again the story of God's
> love in the world; to spell out once more the message
> of human dignity, with its inalienable human rights and its
> inevitable human duties. (*Origins*, Vol. 17, No. 15)

Conviction of this depth comes only to those whose lives are steeped in the love of Christ. How often discouragement and even despair threaten our efforts to teach the Faith to those around us! Perhaps the message is lost on our hearer, and this rejection affects us more than the message itself. Put in proper perspective, we see that it is the person of Christ that must give us the zeal for that teaching. When that is the case, there is no need to despair. The message is freely given. Some hear and accept; some refuse. For our part, we have taught, we have been God's instrument. Scripture offers us accounts of many mystical teachers who were not diminished by a lack of acceptance of their message. Our Lord himself was not even understood by his own Twelve until the Resurrection. It appears that John the Baptist, Paul and Peter were not adversely affected by the opposition they encountered, but encouraged by it.

Since our task as teachers of the way of Christ is in a culture that militates against him, we must have spiritual depth to survive. Purity, peace, respect for human life, and the need for God are elements of our message that are flatly rejected by much of our culture. Because we are teaching not a doctrine only but a *person*, we have no cause for despair. Some reject the person of Christ. As disheartened as we may be at times, we must remind ourselves it is for Christ that we suffer this rejection. He leaves each person's free will intact. He does not make anyone accept him. As true as his doctrine may be, if someone has rejected him as a person, he will have no opening to the Truth of the message we have to offer. Jesus himself wept over Jerusalem when they would not have him. (Mt 23:27-29)

Returning to Christ's message and constantly regaining our confidence in the value of it, in the Person we proffer in our teaching, is a means to sanctification. One must take the time and effort to build that personal union with God which will make that kind of resilience possible. The experience of Christ which inspires us to teach his message affords us a certain immunity from being seriously affected by a lack of faith in the hearers.

> Whoever does not believe, will not experience, and who does not experience, will not know. For just as ex-

periencing a thing far exceeds the mere hearing of it, so the knowledge of him who experiences is beyond the knowledge of him who hears. — St. Anselm of Canterbury

For us to speak a knowledge of Christ, so that others might hear and eventually experience it, we must have the experience first. And for the experience of prayer there is no substitute.

CHAPTER SIX

SIN AND THE SPIRITUAL LIFE
OF THE PRIEST

Morality And Sin

A CHAPTER ON SIN and its effects on a priest's spirituality may be the most difficult of all to write. It is hard for a priest to discuss sin and morality as it affects his own life. And there are a lot of defense mechanisms — denial, false humility, rationalization — that prevent us from recognizing our sins. We are frequently preaching on the evil and effects of sin. We hear about and address sin often in the confessional. We are even, ideally, more attuned to it in society. But when it comes to addressing our own sin, we can be both ignorant and belligerent.

Let us consider the seven capital sins. In reviewing them we are reminded how diligent a priest must be in fighting temptation and overcoming the attraction of sin. The seven capital sins of pride, covetousness, gluttony, lust, envy, anger and sloth are all known to the priest. I think any priest who is honest with himself will find all seven in himself at one time or another. Oftentimes they are well hidden, perhaps very deeply in the heart of the sinner, but they're there. I shall address each one individually.

Pride

THE GREATEST SIN FOR THE PRIEST, like for anyone, is pride. Pride, however, takes on different forms for the priest, and so it requires a little different understanding to be observed. We priests exalt ourselves for reasons different from those of most prideful people. We don't become the elite in a worldly sense, usually; few of us become famous. Most of us are not great orators, nor do we normally have to worry about political or business delusions of grandeur. But our pride is much deeper, and much more insidious. We hold the rod of God in our hands. People look to us to find God. We slowly start to think we are God.

The spiritual life by its very nature must be humble. Anyone who aspires to serve God must learn to put himself last, and recognize his worthlessness before God. This is not easy in the priesthood. "Father" is always given the best seat in the house, the first place in line, the finest gifts at Christmas and he is always the honored guest. What a pathetic tragedy when that honor goes to the head of a priest. The people who offer such honor know themselves that they are doing it because the priest represents God. If the *priest* forgets that, how foolish he must look to the people. A priest with an expectation of such honored treatment is a priest who must be silently (if not openly) mocked by the people.

This is no less true in our time than in the past. People talk about how the priest "used to be respected." Now, however, the respect and honor may be a little different, but no less threatening to the priest's humility. In our day, the shortage of priests means that the priest's time is in great demand. The importance of a priet's time becomes the excuse for all kinds of condescending treatment and disregard, and for pride. It is a real challenge for the priest to be at once in great demand, and yet to sense his basic worthlessness.

The exalted nature of the priesthood, being an *alter Christus*, may be the greatest strain on one's humility. Having a religious understanding about the course of human events, being a minister of the sacraments, having people listen attentively to what you have to say (even when it isn't all that worthy) is naturally going to set one up for pride. In 1965 Pope Paul VI addressed the General Assembly of the United Nations and referred to the place the Church has in interpreting and understanding human history and the human condition. He said, ''We are experts in humanity.'' To the United Nations General Assembly he said this! For him that was a statement of truth. But how many of us parish priests take our little part of that ''We,'' the ''I'' part, and set ourselves up as experts on this or that issue of humanity or culture.

Our fantastic privilege of being able to confect the Eucharist and forgive sins can be another cause for our downfall into pride. As we see people *needing* us for their sacramental livelihood, it is no wonder we become enamored with ourselves and take on a pretentious self-worth. Then there is that great indulgence people have for priests, our bad homilies, our stupid jokes, our impetuous criticism of just about anything. People listen, and even compliment a priest, whether he is worthy of such praise or not. No state congressman would get away with such presumption.

It is no wonder we priests lose sight of our true self-worth. We are too close to the One who makes us worth our salt, and so we lose sight of the distinction. Do not doubt, however, that the people observing us can easily see the difference. We must be always aware that the gratitude

poured over us is not really for anything we have on our own,
but the faithful's thankfulness to God. For without Christ we
are nothing. Literally nothing. Having been conformed —
metaphysically, as it were — to Christ, we are only what we
are in him. Without Christ a priest is less than human. With
Christ he is God's gift to his people. It is a frightening
responsibility to keep ourselves focused, to keep our pride in
check, our place in perspective. We are instruments only.

The spiritual life, the life of seeking God, is the only
antidote for this conceit. Humility is the only weapon against
pride. Rev. Benedict Groeschel, OFM Cap. writes:

> What is the antidote to pride and vanity? Humility is the
> opposite, but it is an elusive virtue. You cannot seek it
> directly. You can decide to be generous. You can pray
> for hope and faith, which are gifts of God. You can struggle
> to be chaste, kind, understanding, and forgiving, but you
> can't really struggle to be humble. Once you think you
> are attaining it, you have lost it. (*Stumbling Blocks or
> Stepping Stones*, 1987)

Humility can't be directly sought. It is like happiness,
the harder you pursue it the farther it gets from you. One has to
understand that it is attainable only as a side-effect of other
things. By pursuing virtue, one will also learn humility. It is
the effect of seeing the truth about ourselves and what we do.
St. Therese of Lisieux writes, ''It seems to me that humility is
truth. I don't know whether I am humble, but I know I see the
truth in all things.'' St. Therese — the one we know as the
Little Flower — does not even dare to say that she is humble.
She only admits that she is truthful.

I fear that I, and many other priests, are not truthful about
ourselves. Like the doctors of the law, we can make the Law
of Love into many different and unusual things to suit our

purposes, and who is going to question us? Who is going to stand up to "Father" and say, "You are a selfish, conceited human being"? Even if someone were to say it, we would flash into such defensiveness, the criticism would be lost on us. We would think, "They don't understand what I am trying to do. Well, how much of *their* life have they given to serving a group of ingrates? I am only doing this for their sake. What ever happened to respect for the priesthood?"

Whatever happened, indeed. Where is our desire for this greatest of virtues, humility? There are many humble priests. I long to be like them. For some, humility seems to come naturally. I wonder if it is theologically sound to say humility comes natural to some, but there are those who seem to be inherently humble people. I suspect those people are not humble naturally, but have gone through the purifying fire of suffering and humiliation to be cleansed of pride. That is what anyone serious about the spiritual life must do — suffer. We must suffer the purifying hours of prayer before the Eucharist. We must undergo the purifying examinations at the end of each day, and before each confession. We must undergo the purifying humiliation of not promoting our own wills, but the Will of God, and respecting the free wills he has put in each of his sons and daughters.

Covetousness

AT THE END of his forty days in the desert, Jesus was tempted by Satan three times (Mt 4:1-11 & Lk 4:1-13). Those three temptations symbolize (in order, in Matthew) the three temptations that normally confront the priest. First is the temptation of pleasure, turning stones into bread because Jesus is hungry. This is not ordained by God, and so Jesus refuses. We can see this as equivalent to temptations against, say, priestly

celibacy that confront priests in their early, zealous priesthood. Next is the temptation of pride, when Jesus is called on
to demonstrate his greatness by throwing himself down just to
have his angels majestically save him, vainly showing who he
is. This parallels the ambition and pride that often mark a
second stage of priestly life, when appointments, jealousy
and ambition become very important. The final phase of
temptation — for both Jesus and the priest — is one of wealth
and materialism: "All this I will give you, if you will fall
down and worship me" (Mt 4:9). In the later years of
priesthood the desire for material security and comfort can be
a great temptation.

All three of these temptations accompany all of us all the
time to a greater or lesser degree. But each takes its turn of
intensity in proper order. The temptation of materialism and
covetousness threatens all of us somewhat. And we can be
sure that, as time goes on and we become more and more
accustomed to bodily comforts, the temptation will increase.

Covetousness is very close to the sin of pride, because it
is basically a selfishness. Thomas Aquinas writes:

> Covetousness is an inordinate desire for wealth or for
> possessions in this world. Man seeks possessions because
> he thinks they will enable him to do what he wants. The
> covetous man will violate all the laws of reason and justice
> to gain money or property. And when he has them he will
> either sin to retain them or will use them to commit other
> sins. (*My Way of Life*, p. 280)

The evil of covetousness is especially detrimental in the
priesthood. As priests, we must be free of the attachments to
this world that get in the way of reason and justice, for each
concession in the way of materialism and covetousness is a
concession of power relinquished to the world, or perhaps

more correctly, the Prince of this World: "All this I will give you, if you will fall down and worship me."

Letting material possessions, or the desire for them, interfere with our relationship to God or one another is tragic. The temptation and danger of becoming overly concerned with money comes from a lack of faith and a desire to control one's destiny. It also comes from a preoccupation with the material side of life. It is a selfishness that places personal convenience and well-being above the call to holiness. And it always involves other sins and selfishness. Storing up treasures on earth makes us insensitive to the needs of those around us; we simply can't appreciate their helplessness. Having money makes us ostentatious, and this is a form of pride that has no place in the life of a priest, yet is often found there. Accumulating money distracts us from our work, the work we should be doing, and finds us preoccupied with our own interests. The list could go on and on.

The evil of covetousness and the way it grows is cause enough to appreciate the need for a spirit of poverty in the priestly life. Grace can flow only into the heart that knows it is in need. "A man with grace is a man who has been emptied, who stands impoverished before God, who has nothing of which he can boast (*Poverty of Spirit*, J.B. Metz, Paulist Press, NY, 1968).

At this third temptation Jesus answered Satan, "Be off, Satan! For Scripture says: 'You must worship the Lord your God, and serve him alone' " (Mt 4:10).

Renunciation, independence from worldly things, detachment, these are the qualities that allow growth in the spiritual life. "For where your treasure is, there will your heart also be" (Mt 6:21). Jesus calls us to renounce the wealth and comforts of the world for the sake of his kingdom. Even if we have not embraced poverty in the evangelical counsels, we still must make it our constant concern not to become overly attached to material possessions.

The pastoral letter from the bishops of the United States on Economic Justice reflects on Jesus' message of poverty in the Gospel of Luke:

> The first public utterance of Jesus is, 'The Spirit of the Lord is upon me, because he has anointed me to preach the good news to the poor' (Lk 4:18).   Jesus adds to the blessing on the poor a warning: 'Woe to you who are rich, for you have received your consolation' (Lk 6:24).   He warns his followers against greed and reliance on abundant possessions and underscores this by the parable of the man whose life is snatched away at the very moment he tries to secure his wealth. (Lk 12:13-21). (#48)

The virtue of poverty, of detachment, keeps one in need, in need of God. One can get tired of that. One has no difficulty accumulating money in this country, even in the priesthood. (I might say, especially in the priesthood.) So the renunciation must be freely embraced and lived.

Just a couple of months after my ordination an older priest took me aside at dinner to tell me something. He gave me a lengthy, earnest appeal that I start right away saving for my retirement. In my pristine idealism I began quoting to myself the words of Jesus, "For where your treasure is, there will your heart also be" (Lk 12:34). Since then I have discovered how real is the temptation to materialism within me.

> No servant can be the slave of two masters: he will either hate the first and love the second, or treat the first with respect and the second with scorn. You cannot be the slave both of God and of money. (Lk 16:13)

> None of you can be my disciple unless he gives up all his
> possessions. (Lk 14:33)

> But you, you must not set your hearts on things to eat and
> things to drink: nor must you worry. It is the pagans of this
> world who set their hearts on all these things. Your Father
> well knows you need them. No, set your hearts on his
> kingdom, and these other things will be given you as well.
> (Lk 12:30-31)

> Watch and be on your guard against avarice of any kind,
> for a man's life is not made secure by what he owns, even
> when he has more than he needs. (Lk 12:15)

The spiritual life of the priest depends a great deal, then,
on a spirit of poverty. Just as selfishness and pride feed on
each other, so do generosity and renunciation. There are great
possibilities in the priesthood for sacrifice. We all have an
innate poverty before God; nothing we have is from our own
hands, but from God's. The more we understand that and live
it, the more we will be happy and free. Poverty and renunciation mean putting up with the uncertainty of life, accepting an
amount of discomfort and sacrifice. Yet, by becoming
independent of worldly goods, we become more and more
dependent on the love and graciousness of God.

Dom Hubert Van Zeller in a consideration of money
offers this prayer:

> Lord, even though I may not be able to rise to the chal-
> lenge of voluntary poverty, I can at least forswear covet-
> ousness. I will try by your grace to endure what privation I
> may have to suffer, and not to cry out in complaint. I will
> try not to allow anxiety about the future to weigh with me,
> knowing that financial security is not as important as it
> seems. But in telling you here of the things which I mean to
> do in preserving detachment of heart I am touching only the

fringe of the matter: what counts much more is what you
will do in me. Teach me where my real security lies. Grant
that my treasure may really be in heaven and not where
the rust and the moth can get at it. If by your help I can place
my whole happiness in serving you, I shall not bother about
the spurious happiness which, as the world imagines, may
be found in earthly possessions. From your cross, Lord,
teach me the ideal of Christian detachment. (*A Book
of Private Prayer*, H. Van Zeller, Templegate, Spring-
field, IL, 1960, p. 92)

Anger

THE *Desiderata* is a short, prayerful address written in this
century by Max Ehrmann. It is an exhortation to peacefulness
which begins:

> Go placidly amid the noise and haste and remember
> what peace there may be in silence. As far as possible,
> without surrender, be on good terms with all persons.

There is a lot in the priesthood that can lead us to become
angry. Frustration in our work and always working with
people are probably the two greatest causes of our anger.
Sometimes we can become angry with ourselves for various
reasons — handling something poorly, failing to live right,
etc. At times we may even be angry with ourselves for choosing the priesthood. But Jesus was very clear in his warning
against anger.

> You have learned how it was said to our ancestors: You
> must not kill, and if anyone does kill he must answer for it
> before the court. But I say this to you: anyone who is angry
> with his brother will answer for it before the court.
> (Mt 5:21-22)

As one progresses in the spiritual life anger is one of the first things that should be eliminated. Some people seem to come by an angry disposition naturally. For these it may be more difficult to overcome. But in most people anger is a weakness of rather superficial variety. Even so, it can be very detrimental to our ministry. Because it is by-and-large overcome early on in the spiritual life, a man of God who easily gets angry demonstrates his unwillingness to embrace even the fundamentals of serious prayer and union with God. When people see this in a priest's life they must be very disappointed. There is no good reason for anger; it is such a destructive vice. And, sadly, it is not uncommon among us.

I know a man (a priest) who tells a story of his days as an altar boy. One evening at Benediction he had given the pastor reason for anger by tripping and falling with a candle in each hand, causing wax to fly everywhere. He thought he was done for. But the pastor did not get angry. And as the man tells the story one realizes that that one event was probably the outstanding incident which led him to become a priest himself.

As for anger, I believe purgatory is to be a special place for those of us who have indulged ourselves in anger. Consider this: Our Lord tells us that "everything that is now covered will be uncovered, and everything now hidden will be made clear" (Mt 10:26). As we have indulged in anger our purgatory may be to suffer the shame of having been petty enough to do so — our pettiness exposed to all. How humbling! In anger we become critical and hateful. We become temperamental and infuriated by the simplest things. If that is laid open alongside God's patient love for us and his infinite mercy, we will be painfully shamed.

It is God's love for us and our love for one another that rids us of anger. As we draw close to God in prayer, we come to realize that his love has indeed conquered all. There is no reason to become angry if we have chosen the pathway of love. Any person who may be the cause of anger is of inestimable worth — including ourselves. To be angry is to think we have the right to act out our indignation or annoyance. There may be such a thing as good anger, being properly indignant as Our Lord was as he cleansed the temple, but our fallen nature makes such anger very precarious. For how can *we* know when our anger is our own and when it is truly God's preference? The truth is we do not have a right to anger. We can choose to indulge that weakness, but it destroys love. It is a sinful choice.

Some think that there is a place for anger, that it is good as an impetus to defend the poor or oppressed, as a consuming fire of zeal for goodness. I do not think a man of God ever has good cause for anger. These evils can be fought without anger. Arming ourselves with love and grace will assure us of purity of intention. Arming ourselves with anger blinds us to reason and makes it impossible to distinguish when we are fighting for the poor and when we are indulging our anger. Our Lord became angry at the money changers in the temple (Jn 2:13-17). We are not Christ Jesus, and cannot be sure our motives are as pure as his were. Zeal for God, to the point of anger, will probably never consume us quite that way, neither would it be thus justified.

Paul says:

> Love is always patient and kind; it is never jealous; love is never boastful or conceited; it is never rude or selfish; it does not take offense, and it is not resentful; love takes no pleasure in other people's sins but delights in the truth; it is always ready to excuse, to trust, to hope and to endure whatever comes. (1 Cor 13:4-7)

In contrast, anger is never patient or kind; it is always jealous; anger is boastful and conceited; it is rude and selfish;

it takes offense, and is resentful; anger takes pleasure in other people's sins and obscures the truth; it is unwilling to excuse, it cannot trust, it has no hope and will not endure the slightest frustration. Anger is vanquished in union with Christ. The answer to anger is love. The place to learn love is in conversation with Love Itself. In prayer God will reveal to us our moments of anger, and will heal us if we allow him. Love one another, and show that love in patience and forbearance.

Lust

SO MUCH OF MODERN PSYCHOLOGY is based on the work of Freud. In a society that is steeped in promiscuity and sex, it is no wonder that the work of Freud takes on such a prominent role. What does this have to offer a parish priest, and how can we interpret our society and ourselves in our spiritual growth? These are important questions. Lust is a temptation that affects every healthy normal person. If it were not our nature to be sexually attracted to one another — the background of the disordered attraction of lust — then the world would not ''go around.''

This is an especially delicate issue because of our promise of celibacy. Not only is the temptation of lust a temptation to sin against the body, as a temple of the Holy Spirit, but also, and no less important, a temptation to sin against our commitment to God. (Just as adultery is not just disordered use of sexual powers, but also a grave sin against the faithfulness of spousal love.)

But adultery, fornication and lust are the hallmark of our society. Permissiveness and licentiousness, combined with pop psychology, have led contemporary society down an avenue of thinking that disordered sex is not really a problem.

Incredible as it may seem, lust is considered in our culture as viable self-expression, a fulfillment of some kind, or at worst a blameless symptom of some psychological dysfunction of immaturity. (Perhaps much of Freud's analysis of love and sex is largely correct. Still, we cannot say that a person suffering from an Oedipal psychological dysfunction is incapable of overcoming temptation and sin.) It is not easy to go against the powerful flow of our culture on this issue. Yet, we need to be clear in our own hearts where the truth lies. Relationships are often staked completely on just one aspect of the human persons involved: genital sex. This is lust. And, as our Lord told us very clearly, it must not exist in our behavior, or in our hearts (Mt 5:27-30).

Within the past year I saw a news program on television about Catholic priests in the United States who were openly living with mistresses. Those who were interviewed gave every impression of being quite adjusted and satisfied with this arrangement. They spoke of the Church not having the right to tell them they were not free to marry. They spoke of "love." They spoke of being accepted by their parishioners. Though it was scandalous. It was a sad program. These men *must* not be at peace. If nothing else, they were not true to their ordination promise. Though there is an element of emotional need, it is certainly a question of lust.

Other, and more directly lustful, examples are people who subject themselves to pornographic material (or, worse yet, professional sex). It is an obstacle to spiritual growth of fantastic proportions, and a great tool in the hands of the devil, who is "prowling like a roaring lion looking for someone to devour" (1 P 5:8). How Satan must want priests to fall. How powerful is this particular weapon of lust in his hands, especially in our culture.

Purity is the opposite of lust — purity in actions and thought. This is the call to chastity. It overlaps with celibacy, but is not exactly the same issue. One can be celibate and not actually pure. (Many are pure and not celibate.) Priests who have chosen the celibate life can find themselves in the habit of being impure, of being lustful. This can cause a great deal of stress and anxiety, because it is living a contradiction. What we are concerned with here is purity itself. (Celibacy is discussed in Chapter Three.) The contradiction is living for God while acting directly in opposition to his will. It is needing the graces of the spiritual life, and cutting off the most basic requirement of openness to them.

The spiritual life of a priest depends a great deal on his purity. If we find we are able to accuse ourselves of impurity in, say, our examine during Compline, then we go to sleep uneasy. If we approach the sacraments, especially celebrating the Eucharist, knowing our lives are not chaste, then we are terribly disconcerted. (If we are not uneasy about that, then we are in serious danger.) Only in having ourselves free of lustful thoughts and actions do we find the peace and integration that the spiritual life has to offer. The first step in the spiritual life is, as St. Teresa of Avila tells us, overcoming direct sin.

There is a definite connection between purity and holiness. As a clear mark of salvation — that is, of overcoming the effects of the sin of Adam by grace — purity puts us in contact with holiness. (Now, purity and holiness are not completely identified. We can think of cases of people striving for holiness but plagued by their weakness in this area. And there are various forms of sexual victimization which are certainly inculpable.) Only in Christ can we remain pure. This is a great advantage in the spiritual life. For, just as the lizard turned into the stallion in C.S. Lewis' *Great Divorce*, we can use our occasions of temptation as a source of grace, accepting and willing to be more than merely physical beings: to be spiritually whole and pure.

This is an absolute necessity in priestly spirituality. The priesthood is not intrinsically opposed to sex — we know some Eastern Rite Catholic priests may marry — but it is to lust. If one is going to live fully that priesthood, one must be, *at least*, courageously striving for purity. This may be a slow and painstaking process for some, especially if this has become a problem. But the greatness of God's mercy, and the value of being truly integrated into the pure mindset of the priesthood, makes it meaningful.

Envy

In the interest of moral instruction and clarification, *Harper's Magazine* asked leading advertising agencies to develop a campaign *promoting* the seven deadly sins: Wrath, Lust, Avarice, Gluttony, Sloth, Envy, and Pride. Each agency pitted in-house teams against one another to perform this public service, to provide grist for tomorrow's sermonizers and to reconcile God and Mammon. (*Harper's*, Nov., 1987)

IF YOU LOOK FOR EVIL in the world, you find it, and not just natural disaster, not just institutionalized evil such as poverty or abortion. You find unadulterated moral evil promoted by people. In a satiric, tongue-in-cheek article, *Harper's Magazine* presented in stark terms what is done more seriously by others.

The feature followed with seven full-page layouts, each using Madison Avenue's best to get people to accept the seven deadly sins as pretty good ideas. Allow me:"If the Original Sin had been Sloth, we'd still be in paradise." "It's time to start feeling good about yourself — *really* good. Pride. It's not a sin anymore." "The only emotion powerful enough both to start a war and stop one. Wrath." "Be all you can be. The Glutton Society. Helping people make the most of themselves for over 100 years." "The world's foremost authority speaks out on the subject of greed." (Santa Claus!) "Any sin that's enabled us to survive centuries of war, death, pestilence, and famine can't be called deadly. Lust. Where would we be without it?"

The one sin that does not actually get promoted is envy. They try. But it seemed even Madison Avenue's best could not think of a way to make envy enviable. "What luck! All the other agencies got the 'plum' deadly sins. But what do we get stuck with? *ENVY!*" The ad is purposefully done poorly and made to look like it is sketched on paper from a yellow legal pad.

The point of the advertisement is well made. Envy causes one to despise the good fortune of others, and constantly seeks to excuse faults in the one envying. Unlike covetousness, envy goes beyond just wanting something of another, or even being jealous of them, because it includes an anger toward the person envied which becomes critical or hateful.

Priests are subject to envy in a particular way. Ideally the priesthood has little distinction among priests. All share the same ministry, the same challenge, even uniform clothing. And often that ministry, that challenge, is not very glamorous. So when distinctions do exist in the priesthood, because of different talents, background, exposure, responsibilities, the natural reaction is to become envious. The fact that only one person can be pastor of the "plum" parish of the diocese, the fact that some are made pastors at a younger age, the fact that some duties in a diocese may appear more exciting or engrossing than others, the fact that when two people work in the same place one may be more popular, all these facts mean there will be temptations to envy in the priesthood. The fact that there is envy in the priesthood means that priests are sinful too.

Envy is a cancer. If we give in to it, it grows in us. It has the two sides mentioned above — despising others' success and excusing one's own failure — and these feed on each other. Not only do we find more and more excuses for why we are not living up to our potential or are not happy, but we blame it more and more on others that we think have been given unfair advantages over us. Envy can be over a simple thing such as one's personal appearance. It can grow to much more significant things such as promotions or popularity. Eventually it grows to be a consuming force in a person's life, causing one to become more and more ugly and hateful.

The cycle of envy must be broken, and it will not be easy. None of us is exempt, so do not think this does not apply to you. Perhaps our sins of envy are relatively small, such as an occasional flash of anger when someone undeserving is praised. Whatever stage of this cancerous development, it has to be constantly under treatment, and it is painful treatment. Envy is something of a combination of pride, anger and covetousness. As such, its defense is a combination of humility, generosity and love.

After the sons of Zebedee asked for the special places in heaven and the others became indignant, Jesus gave the answer to envy:

> Anyone who wants to be great among you must be your servant, and anyone who wants to be first among you must be your slave, just as the Son of Man came not to be served but to serve, and to give his life as a ransom for many. (Mt 20:26-28)

Service means humility, generosity and love. Stop making comparisons. No one has everything. No one is *that* happy or *that* blessed. We have to realize that all of us struggle, we all have crosses, and no one is free from sin. This takes a great deal of self-confidence, however, and truthfulness. For us to appreciate what we have and are — in humility — is a great spiritual maturity. It takes character for a person always to build up others rather than tear them down. It takes belief in one's self to be able to rejoice in another's advantages or accomplishments. This flows from real generosity. Share with others, even what little you may have. By this you will come to see that value of the heart as so far superior to selfishness. Our worth is not in what we have, but in what we give. Service makes us great.

Prayerful union with God will give us that confidence and that generous heart. His love is revealed to us in prayer, and we come to realize what a greatness that is. His love makes us self-assured. It shows us our true value — the value of children of God. In prayer we purify our hearts, learning to acknowledge the things of real value. It offers us the vision which looks beyond the ambitions that naturally arise in our broken nature. Prayer reveals God's love, beside which nothing is enviable, nothing more important. We, God's chosen ones, have no need to be angry or envious. All is gift, right?

Gluttony

IT IS NOT SURPRISING that Alcoholics Anonymous and Over-eaters Anonymous use spiritual persuasion to enable their members to overcome their difficulty. Vice is a pattern of inappropriate behavior that becomes easier to act out as one becomes more used to it. With alcoholics and over-eaters it has reached an intensity that requires more than ordinary decisions to overcome. The individuals seeking to be freed from this compulsion must turn to God for the strength, because they know too well their weakness makes them incapable of "curing" themselves.

This applies to all sin and vice to some extent. No matter what the weakness or sin. Without Christ it is much more difficult to overcome the temptation or sin. But it especially applies to gluttony.

Gluttony is excessive eating or drinking; it is not a pretty sin. Often people who commit gluttony suffer from a painfully low self-image. Unlike the gluttons we may imagine of the golden years of the Roman Empire — those rotund, toga-sporting, wine guzzlers Hollywood depicts — fatness and drunkenness are not a sign of wealth or prestige for people today. People who commit gluttony to the point of becoming fat or controlled by alcohol suffer from it. They may claim to accept themselves "as they are," and certainly God does; yet, society is telling them in no uncertain terms that they are out of synch with the beautiful people. (Like any psychological dysfunction, it is hard for those not suffering from it to understand the problem. For example, bulimic — a term used to describe a person with an insatiable appetite. People suffer from this, but most cannot imagine it.)

It seems, however, that there is much room for consideration of the sins of gluttony that fall short of psychological dysfunction. There are other forms of gluttony that we commit. Occasional sins of gluttony are very common. Getting up from a meal, knowing we have over-eaten, is something we are all familiar with. Or the occasional "one too many" that is clearly over-indulgence. There are subtleties of culpability in such cases. But as with any sin, there must be a direct relation of depth of prayer with breadth of virtue.

For those who are close to God through prayer, excessive eating or drinking should not be. Sensitivity to all our sins is heightened in prayer, and greater restraint to excessive pleasure in eating or drinking should attend such sensitivity.

We priests are especially susceptible to this, because eating and drinking — in moderation — are acceptable pleasures. Our food and drink are great blessings, and we should always rejoice in the gifts of God. But to turn to that pleasure and seek it for itself is the beginning of sin. A priest who has become a connoisseur of gourmet food or fine wines may consider himself an artist of sorts. But a temptation accompanies that art. For when the food and drink become an end in themselves they begin to control the individual rather than nourish him. We have to be especially careful of this. Our life is an austere one in many ways. Allowing our self-discipline and control to falter, because our love for food or drink engrosses us, is clearly sinful and dangerous.

The spiritual life must be our nourishment. "Man does not live on bread alone, but on every word that comes from the mouth of God" (Dt 8:3). There is a need for self-control. Our bodies are temples of the Holy Spirit. We must be in constant training so as to run the good race and fight the good fight. By controlling the flesh we affirm the spirit, and conversely. By learning to embrace daily fasts we can overcome any control our bodies may want to gain over us. The body is good, but only if it is controlled by the mind, not when it is in control. Our Lord gave us the example of fasting and self-control (Lk 4:1-13), and we must endeavor to make it our constant concern to follow that example.

Sloth

SLOTH IS PROBABLY NOT THE GREATEST SIN in the priesthood. We priests are usually busy enough just stumbling from crisis to crisis to fall into the sin of sloth. Sloth is laziness, and priestly work seems to tolerate little of that. But sloth is more than just laziness. It also refers to neglect of our spiritual welfare out of laziness and fear. Unwillingness to put the time into prayer and other spiritual exercises, and fear of the labor involved in seeking spiritual depth, often cause us priests to be spiritually slothful.

Lou Holtz, the head coach of the Notre Dame football team, is a syndicated public speaker. (For a 45-minute talk he charges $13,000, and I've heard he gives thirty talks a year.) There are a number of fascinating things he says in 45-minutes, and among them is his bit on achieving excellence. He says there are three questions that are asked in every relationship: *First*: Can I trust you? *Second*: Are you interesting in being the best, achieving excellence? *Finally*: Do you care about me? Whether his analysis is accurate or not, I couldn't say. But he points up some interesting things in describing the meaning of that second question. Being the best we can be — achieving personal excellence — he claims, comes from two things: having clearly defined goals, and the self-confidence to go after them. As Mr. Holtz goes on about setting goals, he tells of one evening in 1966 when he decided to sit down and write out his goals. He says he wrote 172. Many of them he has already achieved. (Becoming a head football coach in a major university.) Many he has not yet accomplished. (Like winning a national championship. Curiously, he wasn't head coach of *any* team at the time he wrote those goals.) If he can make over a quarter of a million dollars a year just from his public speaking, he has the confidence.

The idea of setting goals has to be radically changed, however, if it is to be applied to the life of a priest. We cannot set goals like those most men might have. We will not be millionaires. We will never be president of a business, nor coach of a team of national champions or be U.S. Senators.

We cannot even set such salutary goals as having a healthy family, our own home, an early retirement, or whatever. It is almost frightening when we think what goals we as priests *can* have.

What goals? To lose fifty pounds? To have a nicer car, or a summer home? To tour the Holy Land? To learn better blackjack or craps? These seem too shallow. What about: To read a book? To have our own parish? To have a bigger parish? To be principal of a school? To be a bishop? It seems there is something fundamentally unsuitable about setting goals in the priesthood. What goals, then? To be a better preacher? To enjoy the priesthood? To transform a parish? To remain faithful to my priesthood? To become a good confessor? Even these have unsavory hints of real pride. What then? To someday be humble? To do God's will? To be pure? To suffer for Christ? To see God?

When a person's life has goals it is more focused. When a person's life is focused, each day has meaning and is productive. When each day is productive and has meaning there is no need for despair or even sadness when trials come, but cause for joy and resolution. Still, what are the goals that give focus to the priestly life? Since our wills are, ideally, to do the will of God, how do we define goals that describe God's will and not our own? If we think in terms of saving souls, or building up the Kingdom of God, our goals are too vague to be useful.

The answer is not easy, but available. None of the goals mentioned above are *wrong* or *bad* goals. Actually. They are mostly good goals. But they are a secondary type of goal. They follow upon the one, single goal that must be at the heart of priestly spirituality: to be one with God. That is the goal of the priesthood. If one is truly seeking to be one with God there will be no lack of secondary goals. They will not resemble the goals of other people in society. To be focused on God and his love means becoming completely unselfish instruments of God. It would mean diligence in the spiritual life as well as the active ministry. It would mean overcoming the fear of laboring to persevere in the life of prayer and virtue. Neglect of one's spiritual welfare would not be a concern for one who has chosen the goal to seek union with God.

If union with God is not our goal, then our lives lack focus, meaning and "productivity." If we have secondary goals that never find their meaning in the primary goal of God, then they will prove empty and meaningless, mere distractions from the basic absurdity of the priesthood. (What the priesthood is, without a direct, conscious reference to God.)

Our goals must include diligence and perseverance in the spiritual life if we truly seek to be men of God. These are something to strive for, but they can be lost. These qualities of prayer are threatened in two apparently opposite ways: by trials, or by complacency. If we find prayer or the labor of seeking God too difficult, too toilsome, then we are inclined to get lazy, lose interest and become neglectful. Or if things seem to be going so well that we don't sense the need for the support of long hours of prayer, we may get out of the habit of prayer and so become neglectful. In the book of Revelation, Christ has John write this to the church in Ephesus:

> I know, too, that you have patience, and have suffered
> for my name without growing tired. Nevertheless, I have
> the complaint to make; you have less love now than you
> used to. Think where you were before you fell; repent, and
> do as you used to at first. (Rv 2:3-5)

CHAPTER SEVEN

MARY IN THE LIFE OF THE PRIEST

**

Mary And The Church

IT IS SAID that if Christ is the head of the Church, Mary is the heart. Mary is a constant reminder of the great possibilities of human nature. She is a woman. She is our heavenly mother. Her place in our spiritual growth is very much like that of a human mother on the level of human growth. She is our comfort, our affection, our teacher. Mary brings home what sometimes seems so distant to us, the life of God in heaven. She is not dead, but very much alive. And she is one of us — purely human, and yet humanly pure.

It is my belief that the place of Mary in the spiritual life of the priest is at once very important and yet puzzling. We go to great lengths to make ourselves conscious that the Virgin Mary has an important role in our heavenly family. Yet, it is unclear what that role is. I find that devotion to Mary, for example, is both highly encouraged, and yet difficult to maintain. Aside from the Mass, the rosary is the most frequent prayer of Catholics, yet I would be afraid to speculate what percentage of Catholics actually know the mysteries of the rosary or pray them.

The ambiguity about the place of Mary in the life of the Church and the faith of its members is perhaps understandable. She is not God, yet she is God's mother. She is fully human, yet she was completely free from sin. Mary is an enigma of sorts. Yet, she is no less real, and no less a part of our lives. There is something obscure about Mary, something very quiet. For this reason my reflection on her place in the spiritual life will seem rather tentative. That uncertainty is an effort to look beyond what is puzzling in Mary's *role* in the Church, to an appreciation of *who* she is.

Apparitions

ONE OF THE MOST BAFFLING THINGS to me about the economy of salvation is the way Mary appears every so often. Apparitions of the Blessed Mother are remarkable events, but what do they mean? Seven of the best known apparitions include: Guadalupe (1531), the one to Catherine Laboure in Paris (1830), La Salette (1846), Lourdes (1858), Fatima (1917), Beauraing, Belgium (1932), and Banneux, Belgium (1933). Aside from Guadalupe, all of these have taken place within the last 160 years. And these are only the tip of the iceberg. (It is said there are, at present, approximately 800 visions and apparitions under scrutiny by the Holy See, though not all are Marian apparitions.) How does one interpret these signs? Belief in them is no difficulty. There are miraculous cures and conversions going on every day at the shrines built in honor of Mary at places of her appearances. Mary is alive, why should she not appear to us to encourage and sustain us? Then again, why? And almost always she appears to children. I wonder why. Presently under investigation are the alleged apparitions of Mary at Medjugorje, Yugoslavia. The children of Medjugorje have claimed that Mary has been appearing to them daily since June of 1981. Why would she continue the apparitions so long? And why only to the children, allowing no one else a glimpse of her?

Mary The Mother

AT LOURDES MARY REFERRED to herself as the Immaculate Conception. This means that by the redemptive grace of her Son, she was kept free from original sin and its effects by a special dispensation of God. At first glance that seems to be naming the Mother of God by an abstraction, a concept. The name Immaculate Conception has one awfully busy thinking of things like original sin, concupiscence, redemption and preservative application of the grace of Christ's Cross. One is so busy piecing the idea together, it is easy to forget that it is a name of a person. In this name, however, we may discover the turning point in understanding, or maybe more correctly, acceptance.

Immaculate Conception is a theological concept. It is also a name. Certainly it is a great mystery. We have a natural desire to penetrate mysteries, to want to understand them better. But always with mystery we can go only so far. Our human understanding is limited, and we are left wanting. We cannot comprehend what the Immaculate Conception means. It is a mystery beyond us. But we *can* know Mary. We can even be close to her, if our faith is strong.

Mary is a person, a living human person, with great interest in human history and all of God's people (as shown by the topics she chooses in her apparitions). As a person, she is knowable. So, if in our relationship with Mary, in our devotion and love for her, we experience her loving heart, her motherly concern, then we have begun to understand. Left to our knowledge of Mary and her place in the economy of salvation we will be baffled. But by realizing Mary is to be loved — not comprehended — we begin to sense in our hearts that her place in our spiritual lives is very important.

Devotion To Mary

WITH DEVOTION to the Blessed Mother so much a part of our Catholic Tradition there is an inherent pitfall. It is that one could actively participate in devotions to Mary without really knowing or loving her as a person. Though that in itself would not be bad, loss of appreciation for Marian devotion could be an unfortunate result. We can see this in our young. Requiring that they pray the rosary can lead them to a love for Mary and the rosary, or it may cause them to disdain and avoid anything to do with Marian devotion.

The first step is love for Mary. Devotion naturally follows. It does not always develop this way, as we have to teach our children to love Mary. But, ultimately, especially in a priest, devotion to Mary must be a sincere expression of love and honor. Once the seeds of this love are sown in our hearts — by meditation on Mary in Scripture and by prayer that she reveal her love to us — devotion can flow naturally from the heart.

Devotion to Mary is both public and private. All of our Marian prayers are written in the second person, thus speaking directly to our loving mother. So whether it be in public devotion, praying as a family under God with a common mother, or private devotion, giving our hearts in silence and love to the woman of silence, either way it is a personal, loving relationship with a concerned mother. This must be the mark of our prayer.

The Church also offers many official avenues of public devotion to our Blessed Mother. We priests know the great variety of Marian devotions which can be incorporated into the Liturgy. These even have been enhanced since the introduction of the Marian Year by Pope John Paul II. It is, really, our responsibility to see that the faithful are nourished by these official, liturgical expressions of love for Mary. And to do this we must first deepen our love for her and thus foster a desire to have all her children celebrating their love for her.

It seems that the ambivalence of Mary's place in the Church, as discussed above, leads us to realize our need to penetrate the mystery of our love for her. We cannot just accept her as our mother and expect that to grow without adding efforts to gain a deeper experience of her motherhood over us. This is nourished by our pondering over the Scriptures as they refer to Mary, but also by studying what the Church offers us in its Tradition. For example, the presidential prayers that are available for our votive masses of the Blessed Virgin. In the preface for Mary Mother of the Church we pray:

Father, all-powerful and ever-living God,
we do well always and everywhere to give you thanks;
we especially praise you and proclaim your glory
as we honor the Blessed Virgin Mary.

She received your Word in the purity of her heart,
and, conceiving in her virgin womb,
gave birth to our Savior
and so nurtured the Church at its very beginning.

She accepted God's parting gift of love
as she stood beneath the cross
and so became the mother of all those
who were brought to life
through the death of her only Son.

She joined her prayers with those of the apostles,
as together they awaited the coming of your Spirit,
and so became the perfect pattern of the Church at prayer.

Raised to the glory of heaven
she cares for the pilgrim Church with a mother's love,
following its progress homeward
until the day of the Lord dawns in splendor.

This beautifully summarizes our love and devotion to
Mary. It speaks of her purity, her place in salvation, her place
beneath the cross, her relation to the Holy Spirit. And mostly
it tells of her motherhood of all those pilgrims who seek their
place in heaven with her.

Private devotion to Mary should be part of our daily
spiritual exercises. The rosary is clearly the most common
private, daily devotion to Mary. The rosary is one of the
prayers of the Church that overlaps every level of prayer from
formal recitation to mystical union. The saying of the Hail
Mary's and the other prayers of the rosary are of themselves a
sign of devotion. Even if one is distracted in praying the
rosary, the Hail Mary's keep coming. This may not be the
highest form of prayer, but it is nonetheless prayer. And it is
an expression of love. Each time that we come back to the
words, each time that we remember that we are praying a
rosary and we try to concentrate on the words and the
mystery, that many times we have made an act of love.

There is with the rosary a calling to deeper prayer. As we
know, meditation on the mysteries of the life of Christ is the
purpose of the decades. St. Louis de Montfort compares the
prayers and mysteries of the rosary to the human body and
soul (p. 55 of *The Secret of the Rosary*).   Just as the recitation of the prayers is the matter of the rosary, the form
actually comes from meditation on the works of our Lord and
Lady. This meditation can foster real contemplation. It is

edifying to see the prayerful enrapture of some which seems
to be afforded by their years of praying the rosary. It is at once
a simple and profound faith, one which can thoroughly
engross one in a deeply spiritual union with God during the
recitation of the rosary.

Devotion to Mary also takes other forms than recitation
of the rosary. Whether it be simply kneeling or sitting before a
statue or image of our Mother Mary, or turning one's thoughts
to her during the day's work, or consecrating oneself to her
Immaculate Heart, or meditating on the place of our heavenly
Mother in our lives; whatever the devotion one's heart offers
her, it is the means of coming closer to her and being guided
by her intercession. Whatever expressions of love for Mary
are made in prayer, they foster that love.

Mary In The Scriptures

THE SECOND VATICAN COUNCIL was convened as an effort to
build unity among Christians. It was envisioned as a truly
ecumenical endeavor. The first step toward an understanding
of unity is an understanding of self. And thus much of the
Council was devoted to ecclesiology. The second step toward
Christian unity is focusing attention on common ground and
playing-down conspicuous differences. For this reason devotion to the Blessed Mother was not a central theme of the
Council. As time went on and "the doors were open" to our
separated brethren, the place of Mary was less obvious and
even perhaps unconsciously covered-over. Today it is generally true that a more traditional, conservative ecclesiology
tends to be accompanied with a greater devotion to the Blessed Mother. (This is a generalization, and as such is partially
proven by the exceptions.)

Marian devotion and theology has always been a difficulty in ecumenical dialogue from the grass roots to the

cutting edge. Because of this it has waned within our Catholic Tradition in the past twenty years. It has been an expense of the Church's efforts to bring about greater Christian unity.

Pope John Paul II wants to restore the place of Marian devotion in the Church without distracting from the efforts made toward unity. He has written his encyclical, *Redemptoris Mater*, to show that Mary is truly an ecumenical figure for us. To do this he focuses on Mary as a biblical figure.

Mary is a person never understood or appreciated alone. She must be seen in relation — relation to Christ, the Father and the Spirit. For this view of Mary the Scriptures are foundational. In our efforts to come to know our Blessed Mother more intimately and to appreciate more her maternal care for us, we can look to the Scriptures to see how she acted and spoke while entrusted with the care of our Savior. I offer here a couple of examples.

The way Mary is presented to us in the Gospels reveals a great deal about her and her loving heart. One of the most fascinating events in Scripture involving Mary is the Wedding Feast of Cana (Jn 2:1-11). Something very mysterious is hidden between the lines of that story (I wonders if even the human author of the story, John, fully understood what is happening in this story). Jesus certainly must have been aware of the need for wine. Even on the human level of knowledge he could have easily known, and yet how often he would be aware of what was in the hearts of those around him. He must have known. But he was apparently not going to do anything about it. "Woman, how does that concern of yours involve me? My hour has not yet come." Jesus seems to have been rather cool to his mother. Yet, immediately, it seems, she orders the waiters to do whatever he tells them, and the miracle ensues. Mary has had perfect confidence in her Son, whem she knows so well.

Mary, seen in relation to Jesus, is all mother. Often, when we think about her virginal conception of Jesus, we overlook the fact that she is primarily mother. As a "young virgin" perhaps we think of her as something of a girl. But as the mother of Jesus in this scene in Cana, we see pure mother coming out. This is so vital to our love for Mary. As often as we may *think* of Mary as mother, it is not until we *love* her as our mother that our devotion can truly become real.

Secondary to Mary's love for us and our need for her maternal intercession, are the two key examples she gives us: Woman of Faith, and Perfect Disciple.

At the Annunciation Mary is seen as having unwavering faith. Her response is not, "The *What* is going to do *what?*" It is a response of faith. Again there is something very mystical that the words of the story cannot convey by themselves. But, in light of a real devotion to Mary and love for her as a person, we can accept this incident as plausible.

> Fear not Mary, you have found favor with God. You
> shall conceive and bear a son and give him the name Jesus.
> Great will be his dignity and he will be called Son of
> the Most High. . . . The Holy Spirit will come upon you and
> the power of the Most High will overshadow you; hence,
> the holy offspring will be called Son of God
> (Lk 1:30-35).

As a woman of faith, Mary has much to teach us. With simplicity and acceptance, she believes that God's word would be fulfilled. And she is willing to embrace the burden of cooperating with God in bringing about salvation. This is a great lesson for us. Half acceptance of God's promises may stifle the work that could be accomplished. We are often unwilling to accept with simplicity that God will, indeed, provide. With subtle pride, perhaps we think too much depends on our own part in God's salvation, not enough on his. The angel told Mary to fear not; and Mary has the same message for us.

Mary with the Father in heaven completes a consideration of her in relation to the three Persons of God. In that relationship, the sorrow of Mary stands out as singular. For, as the Father has sent his Son to suffer for the salvation of mankind, so too has he chosen his mother to share in that suffering. Pope John Paul II writes in *Redemptoris Mater*:

> If John's description of the event at Cana presents Mary's caring motherhood at the beginning of Christ's messianic activity, another passage from the same Gospel confirms this motherhood in the salvific economy of grace at its crowning moment, namely when Christ's sacrifice on the Cross, his Paschal Mystery, is accomplished. John's description is concise: 'Standing by the cross of Jesus were his mother, and his mother's sister, Mary the wife of Clopas, and Mary Magdalene. When Jesus saw his mother, and the disciple whom he loved standing near, he said to his mother: Woman, behold your son! Then he said to the disciple, Behold, your mother! And from that hour the disciple took her to his own home' (Jn 19:25-27). (#23)

Sadness dominates the event, and the Mother of Sorrows willingly accepts the suffering both she and her Son embrace. In the economy of salvation she is not part of the liability — the need for salvation — she is part of the solution. In her motherly devotion to all her mystical children, she has embraced suffering in imitation of her Son.

In relation to the Father in heaven she models obedience and acceptance. Though the valley of tears calls her to great sorrow, she accepts. So, too, should all those who call her mother. Her place in our lives is as our mother. And we learn about our heavenly mother in the Scriptures where her life is revealed to us. She is mother of all those who are disciples of Christ.

Mary And The Mystical Body: A Summary

PRAYER HAS one fundamental, mystical objective: growth in the Divine Life. In the Divine Life, which we receive from Christ Jesus, there is a family. God our Father, Christ Jesus our Brother, and Mary our Mother. We are one. What a tremendous endowment! What an incredible demand! We are the Mystical Body.

We see in the life of Mary, and in our own spiritual lives, that growth in this oneness, this Divine Life, has both depth and breadth. In prayer we deepen our oneness with God, with the Mystical Body, by deeper mystical union through grace. In prayer we broaden our oneness as we realize the great mystery we are — we are part of God's Body, part of God. "As it is, the parts are many but the body is one" (1 Cor 12:20). "May they all be one. Father, may they be one in us, as you are in me and I am in you" (Jn 17:21). This great dignity is unfathomable. Yet it is no less real for its mysteriousness. As we grow in contemplative prayer we realize — we don't actually understand — the truth of our greatness.

The experience of God that persevering prayer affords us makes us fuller members of Christ's Mystical Body. Our spirits grow, as it were, into more of their infinite potential in God. This is the deepening of our spirits. This is the great depth exemplified in the life of Mary. The surface may seem very plain, very simple, but the depth is unfathomable. Not only do still waters run deep, that depth means most of the

water is not observable. This is what we seek in prayer. We
seek the humility to be simple, and our simplicity to be
steeped in God's Divine Life. Thus we are fuller members of
the Body.

Having experienced our oneness with God in prayer, we
realize more and more our oneness with the rest of his
Mystical Body. We close our eyes on the world of division,
the physical world. And we open them on the order of unity,
the spiritual world. In Christ our oneness makes us all mother,
brother, sister. This unity is the impetus for Mary's willing-
ness to suffer, the apostles' zeal for the Kingdom, St. Augustine's thirst for Truth, Ignatius Loyola's missionary heart,
Mother Teresa's love of the poor. We are all one, and as we
come to realize this, our field of vision broadens. We see
ourselves not as isolated and purely alone with God in prayer,
but as part of a wonderful unity.

The unity with God and one another which we experience
in prayer reveals to us our great need for God's help. The
strength and encouragement we need for a genuinely peaceful
heart and harmonious life comes *only* from God. That
fortitude and courage is given us in prayer, and in a special
way when we receive the sacrament of Divine Life. We
priests are so privileged that these sacraments are the ministry
of our life, for they certainly are the source of our life in God.
Like Mary, we live this life of oneness with God in a special
calling of chastity and celibacy. Devoted completely to God's
Son, Mary's life had no division, no obscurity. She is ever-
virgin, and encourages us to a life totally devoted to God,
totally consumed in giving ourselves entirely in service of the
Kingdom.

The unity we experience in prayer leads us to despise
evil, and to hate the selfishness and sin within ourselves.
Though sin was only potentially present in the life of Mary,
her great sense of God — her ''fullness of grace'' — caused

her to accomplish what we might only hope for: to be free from sin. If the redemptive sufferings of Christ have made us one Body, how we must add to those sufferings as we selfishly add to the fracturing and disunity among his members. Prayer must always lead us to a deeper loathing of sin. If we pray and say that we are not sinners, we are deceived.

> If we say we have no sin in us, we are deceiving ourselves and refusing to admit the truth; but if we acknowledge our sins, the God who is faithful and just will forgive everything that is wrong. To say we have never sinned is to call God a liar and to show that his word is not in us. (1 Jn 1:8-10)

As sinners, then, we come to prayer with contrite hearts and a sincere desire to grow in virtue. Virtue is the litmus test of all prayers. To pray candidly is to expose one's self to transformation.

We have a calling in Christ. It is to become one with Christ in his Mystical Body. Priests, as ministers of the grace of Christ and his visible representatives, have a special urgency in this calling. And it is accomplished in prayer, in communion with the One we serve. All of us must take this charge seriously, as we endeavor to be the good stewards Christ has called us each to be.

An Interesting Thought

The publication you have just finished reading is part of the apostolic efforts of the Society of St. Paul of the American Province. The Society of St. Paul is an international religious community located in 23 countries, whose particular call and ministry is to bring the message of Christ to all people through the communications media.

Following in the footsteps of their patron, St. Paul the Apostle, priests and brothers blend a life of prayer and technology as writers, editors, marketing directors, graphic designers, bookstore managers, pressmen, sound engineers, etc. in the various fields of the mass media, to announce the message of Jesus.

If you know a young man who might be interested in a religious vocation as a brother or priest and who shows talent and skill in the communications arts, ask him to consider our life and ministry. For more information at no cost or obligation write:

Vocation Office
2187 Victory Blvd.
Staten Island, NY 10314-6603
Telephone: (718) 698-3698

DATE DUE

HIGHSMITH   #LO-45220